BASIC
GREEK AND EXEGESIS
With *Logos and e-Sword*

A Practical Manual that Teaches the
Fundamentals of Greek and Exegesis
with the Use of *Logos*
and *e-Sword* Software

Richard B. Ramsay

BASIC GREEK AND EXEGESIS
With *Logos and e-Sword*

A Practical Manual that Teaches the Fundamentals of Greek and Exegesis with the Use of Logos and e-Sword Software

Richard B. Ramsay

ISBN: 979-8-90148-116-5
Staten House

Adapted and Revised From
Basic Greek and Exegesis
Published in 2007 by P&R Publishing Co.

The author

Dr. Ramsay was a missionary in Chile for 21 years, teaching in a seminary and planting churches. There he met his wife, Angelica. They now live in Florida and they have two adult children. For the past 25 years, they have worked internationally in distance education, traveling to teach classes and producing resources for theological education and leadership training. Richard has taught for *Universidad FLET* and *Thirdmill Seminary*, and has developed many online courses, including courses in Greek and exegesis.

He holds a D.Min. degree and an M.Div. from *Westminster Theological Seminary*, as well as a Th.M. from *Covenant Theological Seminary*.

Other books by the author include *The Certainty of Faith, Am I Good Enough?, Catholics and Protestants, Intellectual Integrity, Transformed Into the Image of Jesus, Strengthen Your Faith, Synopsis of the Bible, Putting the Pieces Together,* and *Orientation for Leaders.*

Dedication

I would like to dedicate this book to my wife,
Maria Angelica,
my best friend and wise counselor.

CONTENTS

PREFACE

Would you like to learn how to do an in-depth study of a New Testament passage, using Greek, the language in which it was originally written? You may not be interested in becoming an expert in Greek, but maybe you would like to learn enough to use the linguistic tools that are available.

This text teaches the basic elements of Greek grammar, important vocabulary, and the steps for doing an exegesis, using *e-Sword* and *Logos* software. The student will select a brief passage, do a complete exegesis of it, and prepare a written report. The results of your research will surprise you!

To carry out the exercises in this course, the student must have access to one of two software programs, *e-Sword* or *LOGOS*. There are programmed online courses based on this book on the sites of Thirdmill.org and Thirdmill Seminary.

Power Point exercises to accompany the teachings of this book can be found on the following sites of *Thirdmill and LaBibliaaFondo*. (We can't guarantee that they will always be available.)

<https://elearning.thirdmill.org/mod/folder/view.php?id=27821>
<https://labibliaafondo.com/mod/folder/view.php?id=2376>

You don't need to register on these sites, but for *LaBibliaaFondo,* you will need to click on the button that says, "Iniciar sesión como invitado".

I would like to thank the students who took this course in Spanish at the *Los Pinos* Seminary in Cuba, and others who studied with me in Mérida, Miami, *Universidad FLET*, and *Thirdmill Seminary*.

1. WHY SHOULD I STUDY GREEK?

For some, learning a foreign language is fascinating, but for others it might seem boring and complicated. I recognize that not everyone is enthusiastic about studying Greek. Nevertheless, for pastors and teachers it is very helpful to know at least enough Greek to do a serious exegesis of a passage of the New Testament. Since the original manuscripts were written in Greek, you really need to know something of the language in order to discover the best interpretation. There are treasures to be discovered, but many lack the tools to find them.

The purpose of this course is to train the student to do a serious analysis of New Testament passages, using a basic knowledge of Greek grammar and of linguistic tools. It teaches the fundamentals of Greek, without pretending to provide a mastery of the language, and it also teaches the steps of exegesis. The hope is that the student will become motivated to continue a more complete study of Greek in the future.

Here are some reasons why it is important to study Greek and the use of Greek linguistic tools.

1.1. It helps solve biblical and theological issues.

Some questions really can't be answered without examining the Greek text. Here are two examples:

a) "Full" of the Spirit or "filled" with the Spirit?

One of the most debated theological topics in our day is the meaning of being "filled with the Spirit." There are different interpretations, especially of some passages in Acts. Without trying to resolve all of the issues, I would like to mention some linguistic factors that should help clarify the discussion.

Some try to make technical distinctions between terms such as "baptism of the Spirit," "receiving the Spirit," and "fullness of the Spirit." Nevertheless, after investigating the use of these phrases in Greek, it is clear that we can't make such distinctions, because these phrases are used interchangeably. For example, the same event at Pentecost is described with four different phrases: "...You will be *baptized* by the Holy Spirit" (1:5), "...The Holy Spirit *comes on* you" (1:8), "All of them were *filled* with the Holy Spirit" (2:4), and "I will *pour out* my Spirit on all people" (2:17). Compare also Acts 8:14-18, 10:44-47, and 11:15-16. This leads us to abandon any attempt to make clear technical distinctions between these phrases.

But there is one linguistic distinction that can be noted in Acts, a difference between the adjective "full" and the verb "filled." On the one hand, the author speaks of someone being "full" of the Spirit, which refers to a *characteristic* of the person. It describes spiritual maturity. On the other hand, he speaks of someone being "filled" with the Spirit, which refers to an *experience*. This describes a special manifestation of the Spirit, enabling the person for a special task. This distinction is observable only when we look at the passages in Greek.

When the author mentions the *characteristic*, he uses an adjective πλήρης (*plê′rês*, full). This describes a more permanent situation. It is like saying someone is "tall" or "pretty." In these cases, the person is "full" of the Spirit.

Luke utilizes the adjective to describe the men chosen to be deacons in chapter six of Acts.

Acts 6:3
Choose seven men from among you who are known to be full (πλήρεις, plê΄reis) of the Spirit and wisdom.[1]

One of the deacons was Stephen, "a man full (πλήρης, plê΄rês) of faith and the Holy Spirit" (Acts 6:5).

Barnabus was "a good man, full of the Holy Spirit and faith" (Acts 11:24). Here again, the adjective is used, πλήρης (plê΄rês).

By contrast, when Luke speaks of certain *experiences* in Acts, he uses a *verb* (usually πίμπλημι *pímplêmi*, but sometimes πληρόω, *plêróō*), normally in passive voice. The passive voice indicates that the subject is receiving the action, such as when we say that a book was "purchased" by someone, or that a house was "painted." In this case, a person is "filled" with the Spirit. This subtle distinction may go unnoticed if we don't take a careful look at the Greek.

The following passages are examples where the verb is used. Notice that the person filled with the Spirit immediately ministers to others, usually by speaking the Word of God.

---

[1] Where it is not otherwise indicated, Bible verses are taken from the *New International Version* 1984.

Acts 4:8
Then Peter, filled (πλησθεὶς, *plêsthéis*) *with the Holy Spirit, said to them...*

Acts 4:31
After they prayed, the place where they were meeting was shaken. And they were all filled (ἐπλήσθησαν, *eplê'sthêsan*) *with the Holy Spirit and spoke the word of God boldly.*

See also Acts 2:4, 9:17-20, 13:9, and 13:52.

The evidence is clear enough to establish a distinction in concepts, based on a distinction in the grammatical forms. The grammatical difference is between adjectives and verbs. The theological distinction is between spiritual maturity as a characteristic of the person and a spiritual experience to prepare a person for a special ministry.[2]

b) Justification according to Paul and James

One of the most important exegetical dilemmas is the comparison of Paul and James on justification. At first sight, these two authors seem to contradict each other. Compare for example Romans 3:28 (*"For we maintain that a man is justified by faith apart from observing the law."*) with James 2:24 (*"You*

---

[2] Ephesians 5:18 can also be a confusing verse. It is usually translated, "...be filled *with* the Spirit," suggesting that the Spirit is the *content* with which we should be filled. However, some Greek scholars consider that the Greek phrase ἐν πνεύματι (literally "in Spirit") indicates "means" and not "content," and should be translated, "...be filled *by* the Spirit."

see that a person is justified by what he does and not by faith alone.")

However, when we study the various meanings of the word δικαιόω (*dikaióō*) translated in these verses as "justify," we see an important distinction: Paul uses the term in a legal sense, communicating the idea of a divine verdict, while James uses it in the sense of daily life, communicating the idea that a man's righteousness is shown through his deeds.

That is, the Greek work δικαιόω (*dikaióō*) does not always indicate forgiveness of sin or freedom from guilt. In fact, some passages speak of God Himself being "justified" (Romans 3:4). Obviously, God does not need forgiveness! In these cases, the idea is that God is *shown to be* righteous or *recognized* as righteous. One version of the NIV translates the same verb δικαιόω (*dikaióō*) in James 2:21, 24 and 25 as "considered righteous". (21: "Was not our ancestor Abraham *considered righteous* for what he did." 24: "You see that a person is *considered righteous* by what they do and not by faith alone." 25: "In the same way, was not even Rahab the prostitute *considered righteous* for what she did...").[3]

This interpretation fits the context of James better, where he is trying to avoid a misunderstanding. James is trying to correct the problem of libertinism, showing that true faith is manifested through works, through a changed life. However, he certainly is not contradicting Paul's teaching that our legal standing before God is by faith alone.

These passages show the importance of learning Greek to deal with difficult exegetical problems.

_____

[3] biblegateway.com

1.2. You can read more serious theological materials.

Many serious Bible commentaries make reference to Greek words and Greek grammar. The reader who doesn't know anything about the language will be limited in his ability to make use of these resources. Also, many theological books give definitions of Greek words or explain the importance of grammatical forms to argue their point. For example, some people argue for baptism only by immersion, saying that the word for "baptize" (βαπτίζω) means to submerge or immerse. Others disagree, pointing to passages which use the word to refer to sprinkling, washing, or pouring.[4] If the reader knows nothing of Greek, or doesn't know how to use the proper tools to research the point, he or she will simply have to compare the opinions of other people.

1.3. You can discover new treasures.

Even when we are studying passages that are not so difficult or polemical, often a study of the words in Greek will enrich our understanding. Terms such as "world" (κόσμος, kósmos), "flesh" (σάρξ, sarx), and "encourage" (παρακαλέω, parakaléō, literally "to call to one's side"), are full of meaning.

---

[4] See for example Glenn Barteau, "Baptizo: The Meaning of Baptism," July 16, 2014. <https://preachitteachit.org/sermons/ baptizo-the-meaning-of-baptism/> vs. Matt Slick, "Does the word baptism mean immersion or sprinkling?", August 22, 2013, <https://carm.org/about-baptism/does-the-word-baptism-mean-immersion-or-sprinkling/>.

When we study them, using dictionaries and concordances, we open a treasure chest of meaning.

According to the NASB Dictionary, the word for "worship" (προσκυνέω, *proskunéō*) comes from πρός (*pros*, meaning toward or before) and κυνέω (*kunéō*, meaning to kiss).[5] It can mean to "bow down" before someone. The Arndt and Gingrich lexicon says that the term is "used to designate the custom of prostrating oneself before a person and kissing his feet, the hem of his garment, the ground, etc."[6] This graphically illustrates the meaning of worship, to show *love, reverence and submission* to God.

We need to be careful when we refer to the etymology of a term or the words used in combination to form another term. However, in this case, there seems to be authoritative support for our interpretation of προσκυνέω.

1.4. It will be required by some institutions.

Many programs of higher study will require some knowledge of Greek. It's because many of the resources you will need to study refer to Greek and assume you have at least a basic knowledge of it. Furthermore, they often expect you to make use of Greek to explain and defend your point of view.

---

[5] Thomas, R. L., *New American Standard Hebrew-Aramaic and Greek dictionaries : updated edition.* Foundation Publications, Inc. (in *Logos* software), 1998.

[6] Arndt, W., Gingrich, F. W., Danker, F. W., & Bauer, W., *A Greek-English lexicon of the New Testament and other early Christian literature*, University of Chicago Press (in *Logos* Software), 1979, p. 716.

Many denominations also require some knowledge of Greek, maybe also of Hebrew, in order to be ordained as a minister.

1.5. It gets you closer to God's Word.

Finally, and this is really the most important point: It gets you closer to God's Word, and closer to God Himself. The New Testament was written in Greek, and as Dr. William Mounce says, reading anything but the original Greek version takes you "a step away."[7]

We want to get closer to the Scriptures and sense the presence of the Lord as He speaks to us, just as the two disciples who were on their way to Emmaus did when Jesus opened the Word to them:

Luke 24:27, 32
And beginning with Moses and all the Prophets, he explained to them what was said in all the Scriptures concerning himself. ... They asked each other, "Were not our hearts burning within us while he talked with us on the road and opened to us the Scriptures to us?"

---

[7]Bill Mounce, "Why Greek Matters", https://youtu.be/fH8MOb01qJA

2. HOW TO DO AN EXEGESIS

Introduction

To do exegesis is to *draw out* the meaning of a Bible passage. It usually refers to thorough and serious Bible study. The word comes from the Greek word ἐξάγω (*exagō*),which means literally to "take out, carry out, or lead out." When God inspired each passage of the Scriptures, He had a message to communicate, and that is what we want to analyze. We don't want to add our own ideas, nor draw conclusions that are not expressed in the passage, but to *draw out* what is already in the passage. Every time we preach or teach on a Bible passage, the listeners should understand clearly that the main point of our message is based on the passage, and not on our own ideas.

I recommend the following guideline as we prepare a message or a class: Suppose someone hears the message and goes home to tell others what it was about. If they ask that person where the idea comes from, or how they could defend such an idea, the person shouldn't have problems in demonstrating how the biblical passage confirms the main point of the message. For example, if a pastor preaches from Ephesians 2:8-9 (*For it is by grace you have been saved, through faith—and this not from yourselves, it is the gift of God— not by works, so that no one can boast.*), and the main point of his message is that we cannot earn our own salvation, the listener would have no trouble in showing that these verses express that idea. On the other hand, if a preacher's main point is that "faith is believing the impossible," the listener would not be able to demonstrate that idea from the passage. This example is obvious, but actually many pastors and teachers simply think of something they would like to communicate, then they look for some passage to support their own idea. Thus they frequently distort the point of the biblical passage.

When we interpret the Scriptures correctly, guided by the Holy Spirit, we will receive a great blessing and we will know Jesus Christ better, who is the central message of the Scriptures. Exegesis should never be converted into a mere intellectual exercise.

We will divide the process of doing an exegesis into five main steps:

1) Ask questions about the passage.
2) Analyze the original context.
3) Analyze the linguistic meaning.
4) Analyze the biblical and theological implications.
5) Apply the message in the present context.

2.1. Ask questions about the passage.

Throughout the whole process of exegesis, it's very important to constantly ask yourself questions. If you don't have any questions, you won't learn much. If you don't ask questions, you might lose yourself in the vast forest of data.

The Lord often guides our sermon applications with concerns we have. Usually, pastors find that when they are struggling with something, members of their congregation are struggling with something similar. When they speak about these issues, it helps others too.

In a similar way, when you study a passage that you have questions about, the fruit of your study will benefit others as well. For example, one passage might seem to contradict another or teach something that contradicts your understanding of some biblical doctrine. Others probably have similar doubts, so the fruit of your study will benefit them too.

A key aspect of this step is to compare different translations of the passage and note any differences. Why are there different versions? Which one is the best translation?

2.2. Analyze the original context.

God revealed His thoughts in a historical context different from ours, and we should bring the same thoughts into our present context. That is, we want to know what He meant to say to the people who received the message originally, and explain it in a way that the people today will understand the same thing.

The original message doesn't change, but the context does change. Contextualization is the process of applying the same message, inserting it into the present circumstances. God Himself will guide this process for the benefit of His people.

CONTEXTUALIZATION

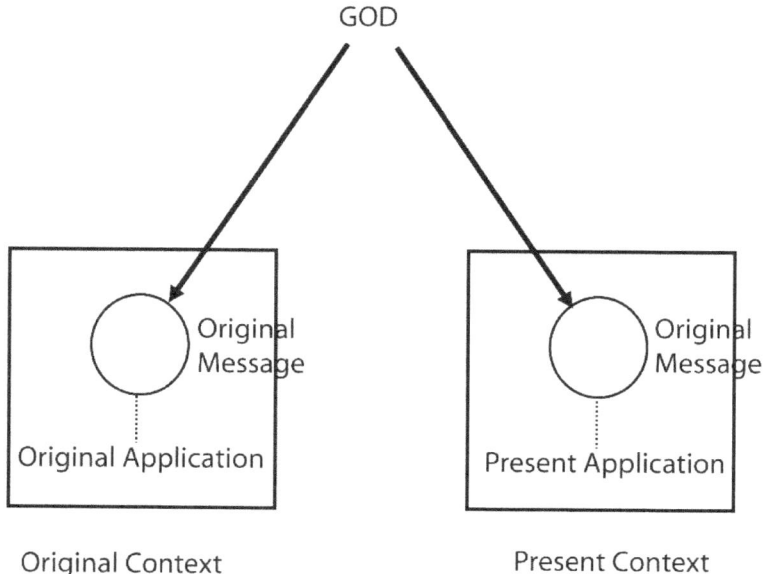

Richard Pratt considers the "application" to be an aspect of the "meaning" of the message. He says that we should try to discover how God wanted the first audience to apply His message in concepts, behavior, and emotions, and then discover how to bring about the same change in concepts, behavior and emotions in our present-day audience.[8]

There are two aspects of the "original context" that we need to study:

---

[8] "He Gave Us Scripture, Lesson 1: Introduction to Biblical Hermeneutics." Video seminary course curriculum, thirdmill.org. <https://thirdmill.org/seminary/course.asp/vs/HGB>

> a) the historical context
> b) the literary context

a) The historical context

To study the historical context, we use encyclopedias, introductions, commentaries, and other articles or books with historical information. We look for data about the times and places related to the passage. If we are studying John 3:16, we look for information about the time of the New Testament, about the apostle John, about Palestine, about the Jewish customs at that time, about the popular philosophies and religions, and about the Roman empire.

When we read about the purification of the temple in John 2:13-22, we may wonder why Jesus became so angry. A study of the historical context reveals that the priests had converted the sacrificial system and the whole temple environment into a dishonest business.[9]

b) The literary context

One of the most common errors in Bible interpretation is taking a verse out of its context. Serious theological misunderstandings are developed this way. You have probably heard the joke about the man who closed his eyes and opened his Bible to whatever page he happened to put his finger on, in order to see what God had to say to him for that day. He first opened to Matthew 27:5, which says, "Then he went away and hanged himself." Next he opened to Luke 10:37, "Go and do likewise!"

---

[9] Alfred Edersheim, *Life and Times of Jesus the Messiah* (Grand Rapids: Eerdmans, 1974), pp. 364-376.

Greek and Exegesis

In order to understand a passage, it's crucial to consider the verses closely surrounding it. Many times, the verse we are studying is directly parallel to, or somehow connected with the previous verses or with the following verses. In the example of Luke 10:37 in the joke above, Jesus is telling the disciples to "go and do likewise" as the Good Samaritan had done, not as Judas had done! We should ask ourselves how our passage fits into the section in which it is found.

Furthermore, we should consider the complete book that contains our passage. It helps to familiarize ourselves with the style of the author and with the principal themes of the book. For example, if we study John 3:16, we find that the concept of faith is key to the gospel of John. (See John 20:31).

It's also important to consider the literary genre. For example, are we studying a passage from a historical narrative, from the poetical books, or from the prophets? Are we studying a story from the gospels, a sermon of Jesus, a letter of Paul, or apocalyptic literature? It would be an error to neglect the nature of the book of Ecclesiastes and quote verse two of the first chapter to prove that life has no meaning ("Vanity of vanities, all is vanity!")

Commentaries and Bible Introductions can help us analyze these matters. Parallel passages are also crucial, especially ones by the same author, or within the gospels. They may open our understanding of the passage we are studying. Many Bibles indicate in the margin or at the bottom of the page references to corresponding passages.

2.3. Analyze the linguistic meaning.

The third aspect of exegesis is the linguistic study of the passage. What do the words mean? Is there anything special in the grammar or structure of the passage that helps us understand it? For example, in order to understand John 3:16 better (*For God so loved the world....*) we should analyze the meaning of terms such as "world," "only-begotten," and "eternal life," as well as the significance of the verb tenses and the way in which the different clauses fit together. This step of exegesis is where we will need some knowledge of Greek.

We will focus on three elements:

a) semantics (the meaning of the words),
b) morphology (the forms of the words),
c) syntax (the structure of the sentences)

These three elements are actually inseparable, but we will explain them one at a time.

a) Semantics (the meaning of words)

Words are the basic materials of language, and often are used in a wide variety of ways. Since we can't simply be satisfied with someone else's choice of definitions, we need to research the possible meanings, and choose for ourselves the appropriate one for our passage. Even if we agree with the translator's choice, we will discover subtle nuances to the words that help us interpret the passage. For John 3:16, we would study the Greek words that have been translated "world," "love," and "believe." For John 1:4 we would study "life" and "light."

b) Morphology (the forms of words)

In this process, we analyze the importance of the *forms* of the words: verb tenses, voices, moods, uses of adjectives and nouns. Here we will apply the knowledge of Greek that we will accumulate in this course. The Greek language has very complex and fascinating forms. You will be surprised at the new understanding that will come from this study.

c) Syntax (the structure, the relationship between words)

Here we examine how the words fit into phrases and clauses, and how the phrases and clauses relate to each other. This third main step of exegesis, linguistic analysis, culminates in writing your own translation of the passage, along with an explanation of why you translated it this way.

2.4. Analyze the biblical and theological implications.

Now try to understand the meaning of the passage in the context of the whole Bible. Take into account, for example, whether your passage is in the Old Testament or the New Testament, the time of the patriarchs or the time of the prophets. Is the passage you are studying within the gospels, the Book of Acts, the letters of the New Testament, or the Book of Revelation?

What does your passage teach us about Jesus and salvation? Meditate on the global scheme of God's plan, keeping in mind the line of history, from beginning to end, with the cross in the center, analyzing how the passage fits into the bigger picture.

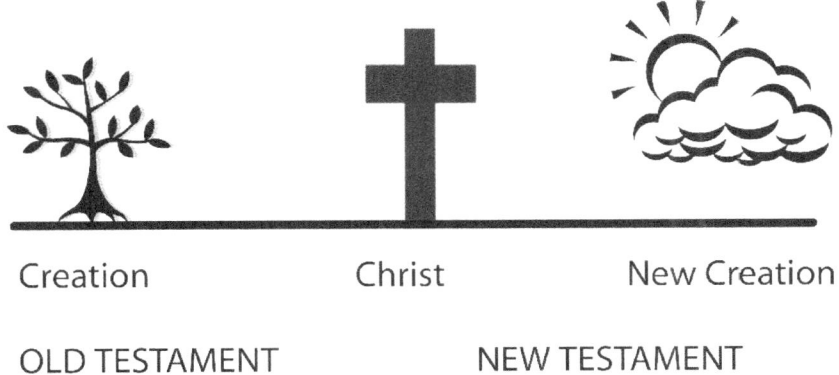

Creation   Christ   New Creation

OLD TESTAMENT   NEW TESTAMENT

Paul said, "I have resolved to know nothing while I was with you except Jesus Christ and him crucified" (1 Corinthians 2:2). Somehow every verse in the Bible is related to Jesus. Resources in the area called "biblical theology" can help us with this process.[10]

What are the theological questions that arise? Does your first understanding of the verse seem to contradict another Bible passage? Does it contradict another important doctrine? Try to harmonize it with the rest of Scripture. Investigate how the rest of the Bible deals with the teaching of your passage.

For example, if you are studying John 3:16, you might have questions such as: If the "world" is all of humanity, and if God

---

[10] See for example the series of Third Millennium Ministries, 'He Gave us Scripture" and Dennis Johnson, *Journeys with Jesus: Every Path in the Bible Leads Us to Christ* (Phillipsburg, NJ: P&R Publishing, 2018).

loves the "world," why does He not save everybody? If God sent His Son to die for people to have "eternal life," why is not everybody saved? What does it really mean to "believe" in Jesus? What is "eternal life"?

If you are reading certain translations, such as the New American Standard, or the King James versions, you might also ask what it means that Jesus was the "only begotten" son. Does this imply that Jesus at some point in eternity did not exist yet? This very phrase actually led to serious doctrinal controversy in the fourth century. Arius and his followers had concluded from statements such as this that Jesus was not fully divine. The subject was debated for years and finally led to the Council of Nicea in 325, in which Arianism was condemned. A study of the meaning of this term in Greek (μονογενής) will be very helpful in dealing with this issue.

2.5. Apply the message in the present context.

Finally, the work of the preacher and Bible teacher includes the practical application of the message to our lives today. Although the original message of God has not changed, the application may be different for us today. If our message is based on John 2:13-22 (the purification of the temple), we probably won't speak about being careful how we act around the Jerusalem temple, but rather about how we care for the Church of Christ, as well as for our own hearts and bodies (See 1 Corinthians 3:16-17).

3. How to Install *Logos* and *e-Sword*

This lesson teaches how to install and begin to use *Logos* and *e-Sword* software. Since software programs are updated periodically, we recommend that you find the most recent video tutorials to see the latest instructions. In this book, we will explain the concepts, but the details may change.

LOGOS

3.1. Download the *Logos* program.
Go to the following site: <https://www.logos.com/>. Follow the instructions to purchase the package that fits your needs. It's best to talk to an agent who can help you select the best library for your needs. For Greek exegesis, you wil need a package that includes a Greek New Testament *with morphology*, a Greek-English lexicon, commentaries, and the "Guides/Workflows" such as "Bible Word Study" and "Exegetical Guide." Follow the instructions to download the program or to use it online.

3.2. Watch Logos tutorials.
If you are not familiar with Logos, we recommend you watch one of the Logos tutorial videos, such as "Logos for Beginners": <https://youtu.be/yt5ZbW-kTwU> The video tutorials will show you most of the things you need to know, but we will give some basic instructions.

3.3. Install resources.

You should open a Greek New Testament with morphology, such as UBS4 ("The Greek New Testament, Fourth Revised Edition with Morphology") or the "SBL" Edition. Click on the library icon. It probably looks like this:

See the list of resources you have available. Write "UBS4," "SBL," or "Greek" in the text box. Select the resource and double click on it to open it in the window. You can look for any other resources from your library, following the same process. For example, you will need to open commentaries, a Greek-English lexicon, and several different versions of the English Bible.

3.4. How to purchase other resources

If you need to purchase resources to add to your library, click on the library, click on "Add to library" and write a name or category in the text box, such as "commentary" or "dictionary" or "Hendriksen." You can see a description of the resource, as well as a preview, before deciding whether you want to purchase it.

3.5. Prioritize.

As you install resources, you can indicate your preference of Bible version or other resources. Just select the resource in the library, click the right mouse button, and select "Prioritize this book."

3.6. Find a passage

Just type the reference in the text box of the window that has your Bibles. You can abbreviate also. For example, to open your Bible to John 3:16, you can just type "jn 3.16."

3.7. Link resources.

We recommend linking the resources you will be using most frequently. To establish a system "A", select a resource such as your preferred English translation, click on the three small dots on the right corner of the window, and select group "A" beside "Link set."

Then do the same with other resources, such as commentaries, dictionaries, and other versions of the English Bible. After linking the resources, each time you go to a passage in one resource, it will go to the same passage in the others that are linked. It's very helpful, for example, to see the commentary on the same verse you are looking at in the Bible.

3.8. Layouts

You can click on "Layouts" in the menu and select the way you want to arrange the windows. You can also move resources from one window to another. Just click and hold on the tab of the resource, then move it to another window and release it. The next time you open the program, you can choose the last layout you were working with, you can choose a previous layout, or you can select a new one.

3.9. Guides/Workflows

You can find valuable tools for exegesis by clicking on "Guides/Workflows" in the menu. "Exegetical Guide" and "Bible Word Study" will be especially helpful. We'll explain how to use them in a later chapter.

3.10. How to compare translations

To compare versions of the Bible, find "Tools" in the menu and select "Text Comparison." Choose the versions you want to compare and type in the reference of the verse you want to study.

e-Sword

3.11. Download the e-Sword program.

Download and install the program. *At the moment, the program is free.* See the following website:< http://www.e-sword.net/downloads.html>Select your operating system. The first option is for Windows (PC). Scroll down to find the links to download versions for Mac, Android, iPad and iPhone. Follow the instructions to install the program.

3.12. Download resources.

Once installed, you can download different versions of the Bible. To do this, find the "download" menu at the top. Then select the kind of resource ("Bibles" in this case) and browse through the list. Just click on the title of any version you want, and it will be automatically installed. You will need to restart the program to finish installing the new resources.

In addition to the King James version and the KJV+ with Strong's Numbers, which should come with the initial installation, we recommend the following English versions, for example:

American Standard, ASV
English Standard, ESV
Young's Literal Translation, YLT

Install a couple of Greek versions as well. Scroll down to find the Greek resources in the list of Bibles. Select "Greek NT" and "Greek NT WH+".

You should also download some commentaries. Click on the "Commentaries" tab and select the ones you prefer. Notice that there is a list of resources to purchase and another list of free resources. You should read all commentaries with discretion ("examine all things", 1 Thess. 5:21), but the following should be helpful: The Jamieson Fausset and Brown commentary, the Matthew Henry Commentary, the Expositor's Bible, David Guzik's commentary, and Robertson's Word Studies.

Add some dictionaries. Click on the "Dictionaries" tab and select the ones you prefer. You *definitely* need to download the following:

King James Concordance (KJC)
Thayers Greek Definitions (Thayer)
Robins Morphological Analysis Codes (RMAC)
Strong's Hebrew and Greek Dictionaries
Thayers Greek Definitions (Thayer)

Greek and Exegesis

Thayers Greek Definitions (Thayer)

We also recommend:

Smith's Bible Dictionary
The International Standard Bible Dictionary ISBE

You may come back any time to install other versions, such as the Hebrew OT and the Septuagint. Make sure you close the program and open it again to see all the new resources.

3.13. Using e-Sword

To look at a verse, click on the book in the left column, then the chapter in the second column. You may want to change some of the settings. We recommend that you show all the windows.

Notice that all the resources are probably linked. If you find a verse in one version of the Bible, then click on another version, it will open to the same verse. The same happens with the commentaries. If a resource is not linked, you can click the little icon of a chain.

For example, you may want to look at John 3:16 and read the Jamieson Fausset and Brown Commentary on the verse. Click on a version of the Bible, such as the ESV, and find the verse. Then open the commentary in the other window. In the Bible version (ESV in this case), click on the verse, and it will open the comments on John 3:16.

3.14. How to compare translations with e-Sword

Make sure you have installed as many translations as possible. Once installed, you can simply find your passage and switch to each translation. They will be automatically linked and available.

However, it might be easier to find your verse and click on it, then click on "Compare" in the same window of Bible versions. You can see the different versions together at the same time.

EXEGESIS ASSIGNMENT #1:
SELECTION OF PASSAGE, QUESTIONS

1. Download the document "Exegesis Report" found in the folder of "Resources to Download". You will use this during the course to write the results of your research.

2. Select your New Testament passage to study.

Ask the Lord to show you a passage that you should study for the exegesis project. It should be short, 1-3 verses. We suggest the following passages:

> Matthew 5:17
> John 3:5-6
> John 4:24
> 1 Corinthians 11:5-6
> 1 Timothy 2:11-13
> Revelation 20:1-3

If you prefer, you can select another passage. (Since John 3:16 and John 1:1 will be used constantly in the lessons, neither of these verses can be the study text.) Ask the Lord to guide you in selecting a text. Think of some passages that are difficult for you to understand, or that you would like to investigate more. Think of something that would benefit your own spiritual life and would also benefit your fellow church members or Bible study group. Meditate on these passages until you sense the Lord's leading in the selection of your study passage.

3. When you have decided, write the passage in your "Exegesis Report," using the translation that you normally use for Bible study.

4. Explain why you have selected the passage.

5. Compare 4 or 5 other translations and write down any differences you find. (See how to do this with your software program in a previous chapter.)

You can also use websites such as "Bible Gateway" to see other translations.

6. Write any other question you have about the passage. For example, there may be a word or phrase you don't understand. Is there something in the passage that seems to contradict another Bible passage or some doctrine?

7. Write down what you hope to learn as you study your passage.

8. Take a quick look at a couple of commentaries to see possible interpretations. (We will use the commentaries more thoroughly in the last stages of your research.)

4. THE GREEK ALPHABET AND PRONUNCIATION

In this lesson, you will memorize the Greek alphabet, along with the pronunciation of each letter. You will also learn about the accents and breathing marks. When you finish, you will be able to write the Greek alphabet, pronounce each letter, and pronounce a list of Greek words.

The first thing to learn in a language is the alphabet. After this, you can pronounce words in Greek and begin to look up words in a dictionary. Fortunately, the Greek alphabet has many visible similarities with English. Furthermore, once you know how to pronounce Greek, you will see many phonetic parallels. For example, we already saw the word κόσμος (world). When you know it is pronounced *kósmos*, you see the relation with the English word *cosmos*. When you know that ἄνθρωπος (man) is pronounced *ánthrōpos*, you immediately see the relation with English words such as "anthropology" and "philanthropy."

It's more important to learn the small letters (in the first column below), since the Greek New Testament used today is almost completely written in small letters. However, it is a good idea to also recognize the capitals (the second column), since they are used for things such as the first word in a paragraph, proper names, and the names of the books of the Bible.

Study the following list of the Greek alphabet. Memorize how to write the letters and how to pronounce the names of the letters in order. You can practice with the PowerPoint exercises on *Thirdmill* or *LaBibliaaFondo.* (See the Preface for the addresses.) Click on "01 Alphabet".

4.1. The Greek Alphabet

		Name	Sound in a word
α	A	alpha	short "a" as in "f<u>a</u>ther"
β	B	beta	"b" as in "<u>b</u>oy"
γ	Γ	gamma	"g" as in "<u>g</u>o"
δ	Δ	delta	"d" as in "<u>d</u>i<u>d</u>"
ε	E	epsilon	"e" as in "g<u>e</u>t"
ζ	Z	zeta	"dz" or "ds" as in "a<u>ds</u>"
η	H	eta	long "a" as in "d<u>a</u>te," or "e" as in "h<u>ey</u>!"
θ	Θ	theta	"th" as in "<u>th</u>ing"
ι	I	iota	"i" as in "h<u>i</u>t" or "ee" as in "m<u>ee</u>t"
κ	K	kappa	"k" as in "<u>k</u>it"
λ	Λ	lambda	"l" as in "<u>l</u>ife"
μ	M	mu	"m" as in "<u>m</u>other"
ν	N	nu	"n" as in "<u>n</u>ow"
ξ	Ξ	xi	"x" or "xs" as in "e<u>x</u>it"

The Alphabet

ο	Ο	omicron	short "o" as in "n<u>o</u>t"
π	Π	pi	"p" as in "<u>p</u>an"
ρ	Ρ	rho	"r" as in "<u>r</u>un"
σ, ς	Σ	sigma	"s" as in "<u>s</u>and" The first form is used in the middle of a word and the second form ς is used at the end of a word.
τ	Τ	tau	"t" as in "<u>t</u>op"
υ	Υ	upsilon	"yu" as in "<u>Y</u>ugoslavia" or short "i" as in "h<u>i</u>t"[11]
φ	Φ	phi	"f" as in "<u>f</u>un," or "ph" as in "<u>ph</u>ilosoph<u>y</u>"
χ	Χ	chi	"ch" as in German "A<u>ch</u>!"
ψ	Ψ	psi	"ps" as in "po<u>ps</u>icle"
ω	Ω	omega	long "o" as in "n<u>o</u>te"

The vowels are α, ε, η, ι, ο, ω.

---

[11] Some Greek textbooks recommend using the modern pronunciation of the υ (upsilon), which is an "i" as in "hit." Others prefer to pronounce it as "yu" to distinguish it more easily from the ι (iota). The υ was probably pronounced like "yu" in ancient Greek, and was possibly changed to "i" around the time of the New Testament, but there is no certainty. In these lessons, we will use the pronunciation "yu" to distinguish it from ι (iota). See William Sanford LaSor, *Handbook of New Testament Greek* (Grand Rapids: Eerdmans, 1973).

You may also observe how the letters are to be pronounced and drawn at the following site: <http://www.inthebeginning.org/ntgreek/alphabet>. (You need to wait a moment for the letters to be drawn.) [12]

4.2. Pronunciation

We don't know *exactly* how the ancient Greeks pronounced their language. Nevertheless, we can approximate the pronunciation of the New Testament times. The tradition has been to follow what is considered the Erasmian pronunciation.[13]

To help the student pronounce Greek in the traditional way, a guide for pronunciation will normally be written in English letters after the Greek text in these lessons. This is not exactly the same as what is called a "transliteration," which uses the English letters that correspond closely to the Greek alphabet. For example, the Greek word ἄγγελος in Strong's Greek Dictionary gives "aggelos" as the transliteration and "ang'-el-os" as the pronunciation. If you only read the transliteration, you might pronounce it wrong. There are no fixed rules to write such pronunciation guides or transliterations, so the forms used in this course may not

---

[12] We cannot guarantee that the sites mentioned in this text will be working properly at the moment the student tries to open them.

[13] In the sixteenth century, Erasmus introduced a pronunciation that makes it easier to learn the language, because it makes a clear distinction in sound between all the letters. This has become the most common pronunciation in academic circles, and is the one used in this text. The question of pronunciation still stirs debate, since others prefer the pronunciation according to modern Greek.

always coincide with what you might find in other books or software. However, they will show you how to pronounce the Greek words.

Since a language is based on its spoken form, it's important to read the Greek words out loud as you read the lessons or do the exercises. Most Greek letters are pronounced as just one English letter, but some require a combination. Below is a chart with how we will write the letters in the pronunciation guides in our lessons.

Guide for pronunciation of the Greek alphabet

Letter	Pronunciation	Name
α	a	alpha
β	b	beta
γ	g	gamma
δ	d	delta
ε	e	epsilon
ζ	z	zeta
η	ē [14]	eta
θ	th [15]	theta

---

[14] Note that it has a line over the letter (ē) to indicate that it is a long sound, and to distinguish it from the pronunciation of the Greek letter epsilon (ε).

[15] When there are two letters combined, they will be underlined in order to indicate that they represent only one Greek letter (th, xs, yu, ps).

ι	i	iota
κ	k	kappa
λ	l	lambda
μ	m	mu
ν	n	nu
ξ	x	xi
ο	o	omicron
π	p	pi
ρ	r	rho
σ, ς	s	sigma
τ	t	tau
υ	u	upsilon
φ	ph	phi
χ	ch	chi
ψ	ps	psi
ω	ō [16]	omega

Special Clarifications:

a. The combination of vowels ου is pronounced like "oo," or a long "u." The pronunciation guide for this combination will be written "u" (underlined) to distinguish it from the υ by itself,

---

[16] Note that it has a line over it to distinguish it from omicron (o).

which will be written "u" (not underlined). For example, we will write the pronunciation of τοῦτο as *túto* and the pronunciation of δύω as dúo.

b. When γ is combined with -γ, -κ, or -ξ, the first "g" sound changes to "n." For example, ἄγγελος is pronounced *ángelos* instead of *ággelos*.

c. The combinations of πν and γν are pronounced "n." The π and the γ in these cases are silent. For example, πνεῦμα is pronounced "*néuma*," and γνώσομαι is pronounced "*nō'somai*."[17]

Read the following words out loud, pronouncing them as indicated by the pronunciation guide:

ἄνθρωπος (man) is pronounced "*ánthrōpos*."

παρακαλέω (encourage) is pronounced "*parakɔléō*."

θεός (God) is pronounced "*theós*."

σάρξ (flesh) is pronounced "*sarx*."

4.3. Accents

Accents are used in the Greek New Testament, and in almost any document that quotes Greek. There are three types of accents: acute (ό), circumflex (ῶ) and grave (ὸ). Originally, these accents indicated musical tone more than emphasis. However, since we do not know exactly how they sounded, we use them now to indicate only emphasis, without making any distinction among the three.

---

[17] Some scholars prefer to pronounce the "π."

The oldest manuscripts of the New Testament only used capitals, without accents, and without punctuation. The context dictated the meaning where there was ambiguity. The later manuscripts began to use punctuation in the fifth century, then accents in the seventh century, and finally small letters in the 10th century.

Syllables are classified as "ultima" (the last syllable), "penult" (the next to last syllable), and "antepenult" (third from the end).

antepenult	penult	ultima
ἄν-	-θρω-	-πος

In the case of ἄνθρωπος (ánthrōpos, "man"), the accent is over the antepenult. In the case of γίνωσκω (ginṓskō, "I know"), the accent falls on the penult, and in the case of πιστός (pistós, "faithful"), the accent is over the ultima.

4.4. Breathing marks

If a Greek word begins with a vowel, the first syllable carries what is called a "breathing" mark. There are two kinds of breathing: "rough" (ὁ) and "smooth" (ὀ). Notice that the smooth breathing mark is like an apostrophe, and that the rough breathing mark is like a backwards apostrophe. The rough breathing mark indicates that an "h" sound should be pronounced before the vowel. The smooth breathing does not affect the pronunciation.

If the first syllable is a dipthong (combination of vowels in one syllable), both the accent and the breathing mark are over the second vowel (εἰς), but the word is pronounced as if they were over the first vowel. Practice pronouncing the following words that begin with a vowel.

ὅτι	hóti (because)
οἴνους	óin<u>us</u> (wine)
εἰ	ei (if)
ἵνα	hína (so that)

Other guidelines: a) The letter ρ at the beginning of a word will also carry a rough breathing mark, and is pronounced like "hr." For example, Ῥωμή (Rome) is pronounced "Hromé." b) If a circumflex accent is used in combination with a breathing mark, the circumflex is over the breathing mark. (ὦ) c) If an acute or grave accent is used in combination with a breathing mark, the accent is put after the breathing mark (ἄνθρωπος). d) Just as in English, Greek sometimes combines two words, drops a letter or two, and puts an apostrophe to replace the missing letter or letters, forming a contraction.

For now, it's not worth investing a lot of time to learn how to *write* the accents or breathing marks in Greek. Nevertheless, it is important to learn to *recognize* them in order to pronounce the words, and in order to avoid confusion in some cases. Some words have a completely different meaning, depending on the accent. For example, εἰς (pronounced *eis*) means "into" whereas εἷς (pronounced *heis*) means "one."

4.5. Punctuation

Observe the following:

- In Greek, a sentence is normally followed by a period.
- Commas are used generally as they would be in English, to divide clauses or phrases.
- A semicolon (;) is used to indicate a question.
- A period above the line (·) is the equivalent of a semicolon in English.

4.6. Writing in Greek

For the exercises in this book, you don't need to learn to type in Greek. You can copy words and phrases from your software program. However, ideally, you should learn how to do this. You will need to add a new language in the language settings on your computer, and you will also need to install a Greek keyboard.

Neither is it necessary to learn to type with the accents and breathing marks, but if you plan to do any academic work, it would be better to have a polytonic keyboard. Although a few years ago, the "TekniaGreek" font was a good choice, the only problem was that the reader had to install the font on his or her computer as well. We now recommend installing a Unicode Greek font, so that it can be used universally. When installing the Greek keyboard, look for "options" and select the polytonic keyboard. After that, you will need to learn how to use it. Look for a graphic image of a polytonic keyboard and download it.

Since these functions frequently change with operating system version updates, and since there are differences between the instructions for PC and for MAC, we recommend looking for the latest information for your system on the Internet. It always helps to watch a video tutorial as well.

Vocabulary List #1

In some lessons, we will study vocabulary that occurs frequently in the New Testament. Practice the pronunciation (shown in parenthesis in the list below) and memorize the meaning. Sometimes help is given [in brackets below] to learn the vocabulary by indicating a word in English that was derived from the Greek.

Notice that in a Greek dictionary, the verb forms do not appear in their infinitive form as they would in English. Instead, the verb is listed in first person singular, present tense. For example, instead of ἔχειν (échein, to have), the word that is listed is ἔχω (échō, I have).

You can practice with the PowerPoint exercises on *Thirdmill* or *LaBibliaaFondo*. (See the Preface for the addresses.) Click on "02 Vocabulary List #1".

Vocabulary List #1

ἀγαπάω	(agapáō) I love, I like. [Among Christians, we speak of "agape" love.]
ἀδελφός	(adelphós) brother [Philadelphia, "city of brotherly love."]
ἀνήρ	(anēr) man, husband [android]
ἄνθρωπος	(ánthrōpos) man, human [anthropology]

γάρ	(*gar*) because
εἰμί	(*eimí*) I am
ἔχω	(*é<u>ch</u>ō*) I have
ἔχει	(é<u>ch</u>ei) He or she has
ζωή	(*zō´ē*) life [*zoo*logy]
θεός	(*<u>the</u>ós*) God [*theo*logy]
ἵνα	(*hína*) in order that, that
κόσμος	(*kósmos*) world, order, adornment [cosmos]
λέγω	(*légō*) I say, I speak
λέγει	(*légei*) He or she says, speaks
λόγος	(*lógos*) word [etymo*logy*]

EXERCISES

a. Practice writing the small letters of the alphabet. Memorize the alphabet. Please take time to make sure you can repeat it quickly without errors, both in writing and out loud. Practice with the PowerPoint exercises on *Thirdmill* or *LaBibliaaFondo*. (See the Preface for the addresses.) See "01 Alphabet".

The Alphabet

b. Be prepared to identify the small letters. Practice with the list below.

Letter

γ

δ

α

ζ

ρ

τ

η

π

ι

ψ

λ

θ

ν

ξ

ω

ε

χ

σ,

ς

μ

υ

φ

β

κ

ο

c. Be prepared to identify the capital letters. Practice with the list below.

The Alphabet

Φ
Τ
Γ
Σ
Ε
Ψ
Η
Υ
Π
Κ
Λ
Ω
Ν
Ξ
Ο
Α
Ρ
Ζ
Θ
Ι
Β
Χ

Δ

Μ

d. Be prepared to identify the meaning of each word below and pronounce them. Practice with the PowerPoint exercises on *Thirdmill* or *LaBibliaaFondo*. (See the Preface for the addresses.) Click on "02 Vocabulary List #1".

ἀγαπάω
ἀδελφός
ἀνήρ
ἄνθρωπος
γάρ
εἰμί
ἔχω
ἔχει
ζωή
θεός
ἵνα
κόσμος
λέγω
λέγει
λόγος

EXEGESIS ASSIGNMENT #2:
ANALYSIS OF THE ORIGINAL CONTEXT

1. The historical context.

Use *e-Sword* or *Logos* or any other library resources you might have to do research about the historical context. Read any commentaries, Bible introductions, and any other books and articles that might give more information. Note the author and probable time of composition. Find any important events surrounding the time of writing. Write down any important information about God's people at the time.

2. The literary context.

Look for important points from verses near the passage. Write the main theme of the chapter or paragraph in which the passage is found. Quickly look over the whole book in order to get an idea of themes, of the general outline, and of the literary genre of the book. Write down important themes from the book and the main purpose of the book. Why do you think the Lord wanted to communicate the passage you are studying to the original audience?

3. Logos

Open any helpful resource such as a Bible Dictionary, the Faithlife Study Bible, or a commentary, to look for information on the original context of the passage you are studying. Just write the topic you want to study in the text box and click on it.

4. E-Sword

Open any helpful resource such as a Bible Dictionary or a commentary, to look for information on the original context of the passage you are studying. For example, you might open the Easton Bible Dictionary. Then click on the binoculars icon to search for entries in the dictionary. It opens a new window. Type the topic you are searching for in the text box and click on the binocular icon on the right. It will open a long list in the column on the left with all the appearances of the term in the dictionary. So if you want to study some introductory information about the Gospel of John, you would type "John," click the binoculars, and scroll down the list to select "John, Gospel of".

Now continue the same procedure with any other dictionary. The ISBE would be more complete. You can follow the same procedure to find introductory information in a commentary, such as Jamieson Fausset and Brown.

5. For the Exegesis Report

After doing the research, open the "Exegesis Report" document and write the information where it belongs. Don't forget to include bibliographic information for any information you've retrieved from a resource: author, title, place of publication, publisher, year of publication, and the page or pages where the information is cited or referenced.

Write summaries of the information *in your own words*. You can quote important phrases in the exact words of the source you are using, but in that case, you must enclose the phrase in quotation marks to show that it is a direct quote.

5. SEMANTICS; HOW TO DO A GREEK WORD STUDY

In this lesson, you will learn how to find the meaning of a Greek word and how to do a word study. When you finish, you will write the different possible meanings for key words in your passage and select the best meaning in this particular passage.

We are beginning Step 3 of exegesis: linguistic analysis. The first aspect of this step is semantics, the meaning of words.

      1) Ask questions about the passage.
      2) Analyze the original context.
      3) Analyze the linguistic meaning. <
          a) semantics <
          b) morphology
          c) syntax

Words can have a wide variety of meanings. This is true in English as well as Greek. For example, what does the word "tight" mean? It can speak of being in a confined space, or it can also mean "stingy" when referring to the way a person spends his money. It might also be used to show how close friends are. The context is the key to the meaning. Remember the example given in a previous lesson regarding the different meanings of δικαιόω (*dikaióō*) and how important the context is to interpret its meaning in James 2:24.

In *Secrets of the Vine*,[18] Bruce Wilkinson questions a common translation of a word in John 15:2. He suggests that, instead of saying, "He cuts off every branch in me that does not bear fruit" (NIV), or "Every branch in Me that does not bear fruit, He takes away" (NAS), it should read, "Every branch in me that does not bear fruit, *he lifts up*." The author explains that when a vinedresser finds a branch that is bent over and buried in the dirt, he often picks it up and shakes off the dust, making it capable of bearing fruit again. He explains that the word in Greek is αἴρω (*aírō*).

If the reader can't look up the word in a dictionary or study the use of the word, he or she will have to accept the author's conclusion. In this case, the lexicon gives several definitions of αἴρω (*aírō*): lift, take up, take away, destroy, remove. Wilkinson's translation is a valid option, and his arguments are worth considering.[19] The point is not necessarily to solve this problem of interpretation here, but to show that any serious Bible student should at least know how to look up a word in the dictionary and how to do a word study.

5.1. Warnings

A word of warning: If most of the translations are the same, you should be careful before suggesting something

---

[18] Multnomah Publishers, 2001.

[19] Verse six of the same chapter definitely teaches that branches that are not remaining in Christ will be dried up and cast into the fire. However, verse two is speaking of a branch that is in Christ ("in Me").

different. Translators can make mistakes, but they are the experts, not us. And if they all agree, there is probably a good reason.

Secondly, as you study Greek words, be careful not to make the mistake of thinking you understand the meaning of a word simply because of its components. It's easy to make a wrong guess as to the etymology of a word. Also, while it's interesting to see the different parts that make up a word (such as in the case of προσκυνέω, to worship, which *suggests* the idea of kneeling before someone and kissing his feet), you need to make sure that the dictionaries and commentaries confirm your ideas.

In the case of many words, they may have originally come from combining two words, but the current meaning can no longer be determined by taking them literally. Over time, the meaning of those component words may have changed. Think of our word "understand" in English. It probably comes from "under" and "stand" in the sense of standing or getting in the "midst" of something. But for us now, "under" usually means "beneath," and to "understand" does not mean literally to "stand beneath" something.[20]

The point is that we need to investigate reliable linguistic resources before explaining the etymology of a Greek word or the meaning of the word. As they say, "a little Greek can be dangerous!"

---

[20] See "understand" in the *Online Etymology Dictionary*", <https://www.etymonline.com/word/understand>

5.2. The Context

A thorough word study looks at the use of the word in its literary context, beginning with the nearest sections (surrounding verses, paragraph, chapter, and book), and extending to the larger contexts (books by the same author, then books by other authors). This is like following concentric circles from the smaller center circle to the larger outer circles. The closer to our text the more helpful.

For example, if we are studying John 3:16, and we want to analyze the word κόσμος (world), first we should see how the word is used in the nearby verses. According to the dictionary, the possible definitions are: *world, world order, universe, world inhabitants, mankind, realm of existence, way of life, and adornment*.

Let's look at the nearest context, John 3:16-19. Each time the word "world" appears in English here, the Greek word is κόσμος.

> For God so loved the **world** that he gave his one and only Son, that whoever believes in him shall not perish but have eternal life. For God did not send his Son into the **world** to condemn the **world**, but to save the **world** through him. Whoever believes in him is not condemned, but whoever does not believe stands condemned already because he has not believed in the name of God's one and only Son. This is the verdict: Light has come into the **world**, but men loved darkness instead of light because their deeds were evil.

What conclusions can we draw from the immediate context about the meaning of this word? First, in these verses it often refers to persons; the "world" can be loved, saved, or condemned. It's difficult to use the possible definitions such as "adornment," "universe," or "way of life" in this context. The only exception might be the phrase about the Son being sent "into the world," which could refer to the physical realm. However, in the same sentence the author refers to the fact that God's intention was not to condemn the world but to save it. Again, the context suggests the meanings of "world" in terms of "mankind" or "world inhabitants."

Furthermore, the context includes a sense of the need for salvation. The "world" is a dark place that needs light. It's not just humanity in general, but sinful humanity. If we extend our study to the way the same author uses the word, we often see this negative aspect.

> If you were of the world, the world would love you as its own; but because you are not of the world, but I chose you out of the world, therefore the world hates you. (John 15:19)

> Do not love the world or the things in the world. If anyone loves the world, the love of the Father is not in him. For all that is in the world—the desires of the flesh and the desires of the eyes and pride of life—is not from the Father but is from the world. (1 John 2:15-16)

See also John 7:7, 16:33, and 17:14-16.

5.3. Studying a Greek Word in Logos

In Logos software, you can do a thorough study of a word, using dictionaries and concordances.

a. Quick Information

First, open a Greek New Testament with morphology (UBS4 or SBL). When you pass the mouse over a word, it opens a small window below with one short line, showing basic grammatical information and the root word. For example, if you are studying John 3:16 and you select ἠγάπησεν (loved), it will show that the root word is ἀγαπάω.

If you click on the right mouse button, it opens another window with options for research. For example, if you select "Search" and "Bible," it shows a concordance that lists the appearances of all forms of the Greek word ἀγαπάω in the New Testament.

b. Dictionaries

If you are studying John 3:16 and you want to study ἠγάπησεν, double click on the word. This will open resources that are connected to your system, such as a concordance and Greek-English lexicons, such as BAGD (Arndt and Gingrich), IGEL (Liddell), DIB or TDNTA (Kittel).

c. Bible Word Study

Click on "Guides/Workflows" in the menu and select "Bible Word Study." Type word you want to investigate in the text box. Can change the language to Greek by clicking on the icon of a keyboard (▦) and selecting Greek (Ω). For example, if you want to study the word ἀγαπάω, just change the keyboard and type "agapaw". You can change the portions of the Bible you want to research. For example, instead of "All Passages," you can select the Gospels or Johannine Literature. Finally, with the prompt over the word, press "Enter". This will open a world of information on the word, showing you how to pronounce it, a list of dictionaries, the use in a variety of contexts, and more.

d. Exegetical Guide

Again, find the "Guides/Workflows" in the menu and select "Exegetical Guide". Type the reference in the search box, such as John 3:16. Look for the "Word for Word" section. This list will give linguistic information about each word in the verse, in their order. You can select dictionaries to see meanings, even see different translations in different Bible passages. For example, if you click on John 3:16, you see the first word Οὕτως.

You can click on the sound icon to hear how it is pronounced, you see that the word is an adverb, and you can click on dictionaries to see its various meanings. You can also see the references where the word appears and identify how it might be used in different contexts.

5.4. Studying a Greek Word in e-Sword

E-Sword is a bit more limited for word studies. However, it is simple to access dictionaries. For example, you might want to study the word ἠγάπησεν (egápesen) in John 3:16.

In one window, open the New Testament version "Greek NT WH+". In another window, open Thayer's Greek Definitions.

Click on the number G25 next to the word, and it will show you the meanings in Thayer's dictionary. You can also do the same with other dictionaries, such as Mounce or Strong.

You can also do a concordance search of a word. Highlight the word you want to study, then click on the little binoculars icon in the window of your Greek NT. It opens a "Bible Search" window, showing all passages with that word in the range you set (Bible, NT, or gospels, for example). You can change the set of Bible books to search, and you can change the version of the Bible you are searching.

Notice that it will search for the word exactly as it is in the word you highlighted. If you want to search for the same word in another form, you need to find the word in another verse and highlight it, or maybe you can modify the form of the word in the search box.

EXERCISE

Practice looking up key words in John 3:16, using either Logos or e-Sword. Practice researching other appearances of the word in the near context, passages by the same author, and the rest of the New Testament.

EXEGESIS ASSIGNMENT #3: WORD STUDIES

1. Find the passage you are studying and do a word study on the Greek terms you consider significant, using either *Logos* or *e-Sword*. Remember to ask yourself questions and look for answers. It isn't necessary to study every word of your text, but only the most important ones.

2. Open your "Exegesis Report" document. Copy the Greek words you are studying and write down the possible meanings of the words. Use the dictionaries in Logos or e-Sword to find key meanings.

3. Use the concordance functions of Logos or e-Sword to research other appearances of the word in the near context, in passages by the same author, and in the rest of the New Testament. If you notice anything important in the way the word is used in another passage, write down your thoughts.

4. Write down what you consider the best translation of the key words. Remember that the near literary context is very important in determining the meaning of a word.

6. NOUNS AND ARTICLES

Introduction

*In this lesson we begin the study of **morphology**, the form of words. In particular, you will learn the forms of **nouns and articles** in Greek. When you finish, you will identify the gender, number, and case of a list of nouns, and you will recognize the use of nouns in some Greek sentences.*

Here we continue Step 3 of exegesis: linguistic analysis. Morphology is the second aspect of the third step. We will also take a brief look at the fundamentals of syntax.

1) Ask questions about the passage.
2) Analyze the original context.
3) Analyze the linguistic meaning.
   a) semantics
   b) morphology <
   c) syntax <
4) Analyze the biblical and theological implications.
5) Apply the message in the present context.

In some ways, Greek grammar is more complicated than English grammar. But this is the beauty of the language! The grammar allows for expressing things in different ways.

For one thing, Greek has grammatical indicators to show the use of words in sentences. All nouns and pronouns are modified to show their use. This permits changing the order of the words without confusing the reader. Look at the first half of John 3:16, for example:

Οὕτως γὰρ ἠγάπησεν ὁ θεὸς τὸν κόσμον, ὥστε τὸν υἱὸν τὸν μονογενῆ ἔδωκεν

(*Hútōs gar ēgápēsen ho theós ton kósmon, hō'ste ton huión ton monogenē' édōken,*)

As Dr. Mounce explains, if you translate this literally in English in the same word order, it won't make sense.[21] It would read as follows:

Thus for loved God the world, so that the son the only he gave,...

The good thing is that, in Greek, the form of the words (the morphology) makes the meaning clear and helps us translate it correctly. You'll see how it works as you study this lesson.

First, let's look at a new list of vocabulary:

Vocabulary List #2

Read the following words, using the pronunciation guide. Practice until you feel sure of their meaning and pronunciation. You can practice with the PowerPoint exercises on *Thirdmill* or *LaBibliaaFondo*. (See the Preface for the addresses.) Click on "03 Vocabulary List #2".

---

[21] See his video "How to translate John 3:16 'literally'" <https://youtu.be/mEojvMRhqHM>

ἀλλά	(alá) but
βλέπω	(blépō) I see
γῆ	(gē) earth, land [geography]
γραφή	(graphḗ) writing [calligraphy]
ἐστί	(estí) It is, he is, or she is
ἡμέρα	(hēméra) day
καί	(kai) and
κύριος	(kúrios) Lord
μαθητῆς	(mathētḗs) student, disciple
ὄνομα	(ónoma) name
ὁ, ἡ, τό	(ho, hē, to) the masculine, feminine and neutral.)
ὅτι	(hóti) that, because
πᾶς, πᾶσα, πᾶν	(pas, pasa, pan) all, every [pantheism]
ποιέω	(poiéō) I do, I make
τέκνον	(téknon) child
υἱός	(huiós) son

6.1. Gender and Number

In Greek, nouns and articles include grammatical details that express both gender and number within the words themselves. There are three grammatical genders: masculine, feminine, and neutral. The grammatical gender of a noun in

Greek can usually be identified by the article. (ὁ = masculine, ἡ = feminine, and τὸ = neutral). Look at these examples:

ὁ ἄνθρωπος (*hó ánthrōpos*) the man (masculine)
ἡ γῆ (*hē gē*) the earth (feminine)
τὸ ὄνομα (*tó ónoma*) the name (neutral)

Nouns are also singular or plural. In English, a plural noun is often, but not always, identified by adding an "s" at the end of the word. In Greek, often an iota (ι) is added at the end of the word. Sometimes, other changes indicate plural. The article is again probably the easiest way to recognize the plural. Observe some examples:

ὁ ἄνθρωπος (*ho ánthrōpos*, the man)	οἱ ἄνθρωποι (*hoi ánthrōpoi*, the men)
ἡ γραφή (*hē graphē´*, the writing)	αἱ γραφαί (*hai graphái*, the writings)
ἡ ἡμέρα (*hē hēméra*, the day)	αἱ ἡμέραι (*hai hēmérai*, the days)
τὸ τέκνον (*to téknon*, the child)	τὰ τέκνα (*ta tékna*, the children)

6.2. The Definite Article

In Greek, there is a definite article ("the" book), but not an indefinite article ("a" book). When they want to express the idea of indefinite in Greek, they may simply leave off the definite article.

ὁ ἄνθρωπος, the man
ἄνθρωπος, a man

However, it's important to emphasize that this does not mean that *every time* there is no definite article, the meaning is *indefinite*. An example of this is John 1:1. The last phrase says θεὸς ἦν ὁ λόγος (*kai theós ēn ho lógos*), which means literally, "and God was the word."

As mentioned above, some cults argue that the absence of an article here proves that Jesus was not God, but only "a god." Nevertheless, there is no linguistic basis for this. In fact, there are several examples in the same chapter that show otherwise. In the very same verse, John 1:1, there is another noun without an article that has the meaning of a definite noun. It says Ἐν ἀρχῇ (*en archē´*) without an article. But the best translation is "in *the* beginning." The context clarifies it. After all, what would it mean to say, "In **a** beginning, was the Word ..."? In John 1:12-13, there are two phrases using the name "God" without an article: "children of God" (τέκνα θεοῦ) and "born...of God" (ἐκ θεοῦ ἐγεννήθησαν). In these cases, as in John 1:1, the name God is used as a proper name. It wouldn't be appropriate to translate them as "children of **a** God" and "born of **a** God." In John 1:14, it says "...the only son from the Father" (μονογενοῦς παρὰ πατρός), without an article in the Greek. Again, it wouldn't fit to translate this, "...the only son from **a** father."

When the normal order of words is inverted in Greek, as in the case of John 1:1 (not "the word was God," but instead literally "God was the word") the first word often does not have an article. This order puts more emphasis precisely on the fact

71

that the Word was GOD.[22] A grammatical rule called "Colwell's rule" states: "Definite predicate nouns which precede the verb usually lack the article."[23]

6.3. Proper Names

In Greek, proper names (John, Peter, Mary), may have an article, or they can be without the article, but they never have an indefinite meaning. For example, Πέτρος (*Pétros*) means "Peter" and not "a Peter." When a proper name has a definite article in Greek, it is translated without an article. For example, Matthew 1:2 says,

Ἀβραὰμ ἐγέννησεν τὸν Ἰσαάκ (*Abraám egénnēsen ton Isaák*)

The article is τὸν. Literally, it says, "Abraham gave birth to **the** Isaac," but it should be translated, "Abraham gave birth to Isaac."

6.4. Nouns and Simple Syntax

Before explaining the use of cases in Greek, we might need to review the fundamentals of sentence structure (syntax). A simple sentence has a subject and a verb. The subject describes who does the action, and the verb describes what he or she does. The subject and verb form the nucleus of the sentence.

---

[22] Roberto Hanna, *Ayuda gramatical*, Editorial Mundo Hispano, John 1.1.

[23] David P. Wallace, *Greek Grammar Beyond the Basics* (Zondervan, 1997), pp. 257-267

We will use "S" below the word to indicate the subject and "V" to indicate the verb.

The Lord | sees .
  (S)   (V)

A simple clause might just include a direct object that receives the action of the verb (DO).

The Lord | sees |--> the man.
  (S)   (V)   (DO)

In English, the word needs to be in this order to indicate who sees whom. However, in Greek, this could be written either in the same order, or backwards.

ὁ κύριος βλέπει τὸν ἄνθρωπον.
τὸν ἄνθρωπον βλέπει ὁ κύριος.

If we simply read the words of the second version literally in order, without understanding Greek grammar, we might think it says, "The man sees the Lord." However, after learning the use of cases in Greek, we know that it means "The Lord sees the man."

Many times there is also an *indirect object* that receives an *indirect* effect of the action. For example, in the sentence "The man bought me a book," "me" is the indirect object (IO), while "a book" is the direct object (DO).

Greek and Exegesis

```
                (IO)
                me
                 /
 The man    bought  |--> a book
   (S)        (V)        (DO)
```

In Greek, our understanding of cases will help us identify a direct object and an indirect object.

6.5. Cases

There are five cases in Greek. We will give an example of each case, using the same noun, ἀδελφὸς ("brother"):

a. *Nominative* - when the noun is used as a subject or as a predicate nominative (explained in a section below).

> ὁ ἀδελφὸς βλέπει τόν υἱόν.
> (*ho adelphós blépei ton huión*)
> The brother sees the son.

b. *Genitive* - when the noun is used to express possession.

> ὁ ἄνθρωπος βλέπει τὸν υἱὸν τοῦ ἀδελφοῦ.
> (*ho ánthrōpos blépei ton huión tu adelphú*)
> The man sees the son of the brother.

c. *Dative* - when the noun is used as an indirect object.

> ὁ ἄνθρωπος λέγει λόγον τῷ ἀδελφῷ.

74

(*ho án<u>th</u>rōpos légei lógon tō adelphō´*)
The man says a word <u>to the brother</u>.

d. *Accusative* - when the noun is used as a direct object.

ὁ υἱὸς βλέπει <u>τὸν ἀδελφόν</u>.
(*ho huiós blépei ton adel<u>phón</u>*)
The son sees <u>the brother</u>.

e. *Vocative* - when a person is spoken to directly.

ὁ ἄνθρωπος λέγει λόγον, <u>ἀδελφέ</u>.
(*ho án<u>th</u>rōpos légei lógon, adelphé*)
The man speaks (or says) a word, <u>brother</u>.

6.6. The "Declension" of the Article

As mentioned above, the article is the best sign of case, gender, and number of a noun. The following table demonstrates the forms of the article in all cases (except vocative) and genders, singular and plural. This list of forms is called the "declension" of the article.

Singular

Case	Masc	Fem	Neutral
Nom	ὁ	ἡ	τό
Gen	τοῦ	τῆς	τοῦ

Dat	τῷ	τῇ	τῷ
Acus	τόν	τήν	τό

Plural

Case	Masc	Fem	Neutral
Nom	οἱ	αἱ	τά
Gen	τῶν	τῶν	τῶν
Dat	τοῖς	ταῖς	τοῖς
Acus	τούς	τάς	τά

Note that the forms of dative singular have a small iota (ι) under the letters ω and η. This is called the "iota subscript," and it does not change the pronunciation of the letter.

6.7. The Declension of Some Nouns

The following tables show the forms of some nouns in all their cases, in singular and plural, accompanied by the article. The list of forms of a noun is called the "declension" of the noun. The translations given below are common, but they might change according to the context.

ὁ ἀδελφός (*ho adelphós*) the brother

SING

Nom	**ὁ ἀδελφός** (*ho adelphós*)	the brother
Gen	**τοῦ ἀδελφοῦ** (*tu adelphú*)	of the brother
Dat	**τῷ ἀδελφῷ** (*tō adelphō´*)	to/for the brother
Acc	**τὸν ἀδελφόν** (*ton adelphón*)	the brother
Voc	**ἀδελφέ** (*adelphé*)	Brother!

PL

Nom	**οἱ ἀδελφοί** (*hoi adelphói*)	the brothers
Gen	**τῶν ἀδελφῶν** (*tōn adelphō´n*)	of the brothers
Dat	**τοῖς ἀδελφοῖς** (*tois adelphóis*)	for the brothers
Acc	**τοὺς ἀδελφούς** (*tus adelphu´s*)	the brothers
Voc	**ἀδελφοί** (*adelphói*)	Brothers!

Greek and Exegesis

τό τὲκνον (*to téknon*) the child

SING

Nom	τὸ τέκνον	the child
	(*to téknon*)	
Gen	τοῦ τέκνου	of the child
	(*tu téknu*)	
Dat	τῷ τέκνῳ	to/for the child
	(*tō téknō*)	
Acc	τὸ τέκνον	the child
	(*to téknon*)	
Voc	τέκνον	Child!
	(*téknon*)	

PL

Nom	τὰ τέκνα	the children
	(*ta tékna*)	
Gen	τῶν τέκνων	of the children
	(*tōn téknōn*)	
Dat	τοῖς τέκνοις	for the children
	(*tois téknois*)	
Acc	τὰ τέκνα	the children
	(*ta tékna*)	
Voc	τέκνα	Children!
	(*tékna*)	

ἡ γραφή (*hē graphē*) the writing

SING

Nom	**ἡ γραφή** (*hē graphḗ*)	the writing
Gen	**τῆς γραφῆς** (*tēs graphḗs*)	of the writing
Dat	**τῇ γραφῇ** (*tē graphḗ*)	for the writing
Acc	**τὴν γραφήν** (*tēn graphḗn*)	the writing
Voc	**γραφή** (*graphḗ*)	Writing!

PL

Nom	**αἱ γραφαί** (*hai graphái*)	the writings
Gen	**τῶν γραφῶν** (*tōn graphō̃n*)	of the writings
Dat	**ταῖς γραφαῖς** (*tais grapháis*)	for the writings
Acc	**τὰς γραφάς** (*tas graphás*)	the writings
Voc	**γραφαί** (*graphái*)	Writings!

6.8. The Predicate Nominative

When a noun is used after a form of the verb "to be," it is called a predicate nominative (PrNom).

The man **is** a <u>brother</u>.
        (PrNom)

In Greek, the predicate nominative is in the nominative case, like the subject. The verb "to be" in Greek is εἰμί (*eimí*, I am). In third person singular, the verb is ἐστί (*estí*: it, he, or she is).

ὁ ἄνθρωπος ἐστὶ ἀδελφός.
(*ho ánthrōpos estí adelphós*)
The man is a <u>brother</u>.

Matthew 16:16 contains an example of a predicate nominative. Peter confesses to Jesus, "You are the Christ" (Σὺ εἶ ὁ Χριστὸς). "You" (Σὺ) is the subject, "are" (εἶ) is the verb, and "the Christ" (ὁ Χριστὸς) is the predicate nominative.

6.9. Recognizing the Forms

It's difficult to memorize all the possible forms of nouns. Therefore, it's good to know how to *recognize* the pointers to gender, number, and case. These are not always obvious, but there are many guidelines that help. The most obvious forms are the genitive and dative. If you see a noun that ends in -ων, you assume that it corresponds to genitive plural. If you find a noun that ends in -ου you can assume that it is genitive singular. If you see a noun that ends in -ῳ, or ῃ, you can assume that it is dative singular. Here the clue is the small iota subscript. If you find a noun that ends in -οις or -αις, yo can assume it is dative plural. Normally the article and the context will help to identify the case, gender, and number of the nouns, but when you encounter a form that you don't recognize, you can look it up in programs like *Logos* or *e-Sword*.

EXERCISES

You can practice with the PowerPoint exercises on *Thirdmill* or *LaBibliaaFondo.* (See the Preface for the addresses. Click on "04 Nouns and Articles". Then do the following exercises.

a. Memorize the forms of the definite article.

It is helpful to at least know the forms of the definite article, since it indicates the gender, case, and number of the noun that it precedes.

Singular

Case	Masc	Fem	Neutral
Nom	ὁ	ἡ	τό
Gen	τοῦ	τῆς	τοῦ
Dat	τῷ	τῇ	τῷ
Acus	τόν	τήν	τό

81

Plural

Case	Masc	Fem	Neutral
Nom	οἱ	αἱ	τά
Gen	τῶν	τῶν	τῶν
Dat	τοῖς	ταῖς	τοῖς
Acus	τούς	τάς	τά

b. Know the principal use of each case:

nominative case
genitive case
dative case
accusative case
vocative case

c. Be able to identify the gender, number, and case of the following nouns. (In some cases there may be more than one possibility). Try to find clues in the articles, but if you are not sure, look up the words in the section on declensions above. Again, remember to practice with the PowerPoint presentations.

Nouns and Articles

	Gender	Number	Case
οἱ ἀδελφοί			
τοῦ ἀδελφοῦ			
τῶν ἀδελφῶν			
τὸ τέκνον			
τὰ τέκνα			
τοῖς τέκνοις			
τῇ γραφῇ			
τῶν γραφῶν			
ταῖς γραφαῖς			
τῆς γραφῆς			

d. Practice analyzing the use of nouns in a sentence. First, we will use English sentences, then Greek sentences.

- Identify the nouns and the verbs in the following sentences (both English and Greek). Put an "S" below a subject, "V" below a verb, "DO" below a direct object, "IO" under an indirect object, "PrNom" below a predicate nominative, and "Poss" under a noun or phrase in its possessive form.
- Indicate the case of each noun in the Greek sentences (Nom, Accus, Dat. Gen).
- Translate the Greek sentences into English. You should be able to do this if you have learned the vocabulary from lists #1 and #2.

1) The teacher bought me a book.

2) The <u>student</u> <u>is</u> the <u>brother</u> <u>of the man</u>.

3) ὁ ἄνθρωπος λέγει λόγον τῷ ἀδελφῷ.

4) ὁ ἀδελφός ἐστιν ὁ μαθητῆς.

5) τὸν ἄνθρωπον βλέπει ὁ κύριος.

6) βλέπω τὸ τέκνον τοῦ ἀδελφοῦ.

7) τῷ ἀδελφῷ λέγει ὄνομα ὁ υἱός.

You can practice with the PowerPoint exercises on *Thirdmill* or *LaBibliaaFondo.* (See the Preface for the addresses.) Click on "04 Nouns and Articles".

EXEGESIS ASSIGNMENT #4: ANALYSIS OF NOUNS

Using *Logos*

1. If you are using *Logos* software, you can select the "Guides/Workflows" and open the "Exegetical Guide." Enter the reference to the passage you are studying in the text box, then scroll down to the "Word by Word" information.

2. Find all the important nouns in your passages and write down the information in the "Exegesis Report."

3. Make a list by copying them from your passage in Greek. Note the case, number and (grammatical) gender of each one.

4. Write also the use they have in the sentence: subject, direct object, indirect object, or predicate nominative.

5. You may want to look at a dictionary again to consider how the important nouns should be translated in your passage.

Using *e-Sword*

1. If you are using *e-Sword*, you can open the version of the Greek New Testament "Greek NT WH+". Look at the blue codes just above the Greek words and identify the nouns. Open *Robinson's Morphological Analysis Codes* (RMAC) in another window. When you click on any blue code in the Greek verse, you can find the information in the RMAC.

2. Enter the following information in your "Exegesis Report":

Greek and Exegesis

a. Make a list of important nouns by copying them from your passage in Greek.

b. Note the case, number and (grammatical) gender of each one.

c. Write also the use they have in the sentence: subject, direct object, indirect object, or predicate nominative.

3. You may want to look at a dictionary again to consider how the important nouns should be translated in your passage.

7. ADJECTIVES, ADVERBS, PRONOUNS AND PREPOSITIONS

In this lesson, you will continue to study Greek words, focusing now on adjectives, adverbs, pronouns, and prepositions. When you finish, you will identify the adjectives, adverbs, pronouns, and prepositions in some sample sentences in both English and Greek, as well as in your own passage for study.

It's essential to recognize the meaning of these words and their use in a sentence. For example, in John 3:16, the first word οὕτως ("thus" or "in this manner") is an important adverb, because it points to *how* God showed His love. (Notice that in English the word order is changed.) Since οὕτως is often translated "so", we might initially think the author is saying, "God loved the world *so much* that...". However that's not exactly what he is saying; he is not saying how *much* He loved the world, but in what *manner* He showed His love, by giving His Son.

As another example, suppose you are reading a commentary like *Robertson's Word Pictures* on John 1:1 that mentions the grammatical importance of the preposition in the phrase, "the word was *with* God" (πρὸς τὸν θεόν, *pros ton theón*). He says:

> Though existing eternally with God, the Word was in perfect fellowship with God. *Pros* with the accusative presents a plane of equality and intimacy, face to face with each other.[24]

Why does he mention that the Greek word pros (πρὸς) has a certain meaning *with the accusative*? This is one of the grammatical points we will study in this chapter. First, let's learn some new vocabulary:

Vocabulary List #3, Part A

Learn this list of vocabulary. Pronounce them over and over, using the help of the pronunciation guides in parentheses, until you are sure you can pronounce them correctly. Memorize the meaning of each word. You can practice with the PowerPoint exercises on *Thirdmill* or *LaBibliaaFondo.* (See the Preface for the addresses.) Click on "05 Vocabulary List #3".

ἄγιος	(*hágios*) holy (*hagio*graphs, Hebrew holy writings)
αἰών	(*aiō´n*) age, eon, epoch
αἰώνιος	(*aiō´nios*) eternal
αὐτός, αὐτή, αὐτό	(*autós, autē´, autó*) he, she, it, himself, herself, itself
γινώσκω	(*ginō´skō*) I know (*gno*sticism)
γυνή	(*gunē´*) woman, wife

---

[24] Robertson, *A. Robertson's Word Pictures in Six Volumes* (electronic ed.), *Logos Software.*

	(gynecology)
δίδωμι	(*dídōmi*) I give
δύναμαι	(*dúnamai*) I can (*dyna*mite)
ἐγώ	(*egō´*) I (*ego*centric)
ἐκεῖνος	(*ekéinos*) that
ἔρχομαι	(ér<u>ch</u>omai) I come, I go
ἐξέρχομαι	(exér<u>ch</u>omai) I leave
ἤ	(*ē*) or (Note the breathing mark to distinguish this word from the feminine article ἡ)
κατά	(*katá*) against, according to, during
λαλέω	(*laléō*) I speak
μή	(*mē*) no
μόνον	(*mónon*) only
νῦν	(*nun*) now
οὐ	(<u>u</u>) no
πιστεύω	(*pistéuō*) I believe
σύ	(*su*) you
οὐρανός	(<u>u</u>*ranós*) heaven
οὗτος, αὕτη, τοῦτο	(h<u>u</u>*tos*, h*áutē*, t<u>ú</u>*to*) this
οὕτως	(h<u>ú</u>*tōs*) thus

7.1. Adjectives

Look at a phrase in Revelation 4:8 in Greek:

Ἅγιος ἅγιος ἅγιος κύριος ὁ Θεὸς ὁ παντοκράτωρ
(*hágios, hágios, hágios, kúrios ho theós ho pantocrátōr*)
Holy, holy, holy, is the Lord God almighty!

Notice that the words for "holy" (ἁγιος) have the same ending (-ος) as "Lord" (Κύριος) and "God" (Θεὸς). This is a grammatical pattern in Greek; the adjectives normally coincide with the nouns they modify in gender, number and case. If you use software such as *Logos* to analyze this word, it will say ἁγιος is an "adjective, masculine, singular, nominative."

In English, adjectives don't change with the noun they modify.

The book is *big*.
The books are *big*.

However, in Greek, the adjective must agree with the noun in its gender, number, and case. In the following example, the subject οἱ ἀδελφοὶ (the brothers) is **masculine plural nominative**, so the adjective (ἁγιοι) must correspond.

οἱ ἀδελφοὶ εἰσὶν **ἁγιοι**.
(*hoi adelphói eisín hágioi*)
The brothers are holy.

The adjective can be either between the article and the noun, or it can also come after the noun it modifies, with another article in front of it.

ἐστὶν ὁ ἀδελφὸς **τοῦ ἁγίου ἀνθρώπου**.
(*estín ho adelphós tu hagíu anthrṓpu.*)
He is the brother of the holy man.

ἐστὶν ὁ ἀδελφὸς **τοῦ ἀνθρώπου τοῦ ἁγίου**.
(*estín ho adelphós tu anthrṓpu tu hagíu.*)
He is the brother of the holy man.

In the second case, more emphasis is on the adjective. (He is the brother of the man, that is the man who is *holy*.)
An adjective can also be used as a noun.

ὁ ἅγιος ἐστὶν ὁ ἀδελφός μοῦ.
(*ho hágios estín ho adelphós mu.*)
The holy one (or holy man) is my brother.

7.2. Adverbs

Adverbs modify verbs. In the following sentence, "quickly" is an adverb, because it tells something about the action of buying the book.

He bought the book *quickly*.

Greek and Exegesis

The diagram is as follows:

He | bought |--> the book.
        ⎩quickly

In John 3:16, Οὕτως (thus) is an adverb.

Οὕτως γὰρ ἠγάπησεν ὁ θεὸς τὸν κόσμον
(*Hútōs gar ēgápēsen ho theós ton kósmon*)
Thus for loved God the world...

The following are a few common Greek adverbs:

μή   (*mē*) no
μόνον (*mónon*) only
νῦν   (*nun*) now
οὐ   (*u*) no
οὕτως (*hútōs*) thus

7.3. Pronouns

Pronouns replace nouns. ("Man" is a noun, and "he" is a pronoun that may replace it.) In Greek, the pronouns also change according to number and case.

Observe the following tables of personal pronouns. It's not necessary to memorize them, but try to notice some of the clues for recognizing them. Some of the endings are very similar to the article. Notice that -ου indicates genitive singular, -ι indicates dative singular (sometimes it is an iota subscript as in ῳ and ῃ), and ων indicates genitive plural, for example.

First Person (I, we)

SING		Pronounce	Translate
N.	ἐγώ	egō´	I
G.	ἐμοῦ / μου	emu̱ / mu̱	my
D.	ἐμοί / μοι	emói / moi	for me
A.	ἐμέ / με	emé / me	me
PL.			
N.	ἡμεῖς	hēméis	we
G.	ἡμῶν	hēmō´n	our
D.	ἡμῖν	hēmín	for us
A.	ἡμᾶς	hēmás	us

Second Person (You)

SING		Pronounce	Translate
N.	σύ	su	you
G.	σοῦ	su̱	your
D.	σοί	soi	for you
A.	σέ	sé	you
PL			
N.	ὑμεῖς	huméis	you
G.	ὑμῶν	humō´n	your
D.	ὑμῖν	humín	for you
A.	ὑμᾶς	humás	you

The third person pronoun also changes according to its gender, as well as case and number.

Third person (he, she, it, they)

SING	Masc	Fem	Neutral
N.	αὐτός he	αὐτή she	αὐτό it
G.	αὐτοῦ his	αὐτῆς her	αὐτοῦ its
D.	αὐτῷ for him	αὐτῇ for her	αὐτῷ for it
A.	αὐτόν him	αὐτήν her	αὐτό it
PL			
N.	αὐτοί they	αὐται they	αὐτά they
G.	αὐτῶν their	αὐτῶν their	αὐτῶν their
D.	αὐτοῖς for them	αὐταῖς for them	αὐτοῖς for them
A.	αὐτούς them	αὐτάς them	αὐτά them

7.4. Prepositions

The preposition joins a noun or pronoun to form a phrase that relates to the rest of the sentence. Its very name indicates that it is in a position before the word that it connects. A phrase that contains a preposition can modify a noun or a verb, and is called a prepositional phrase.

He lives *in* a house.
("In" is the preposition. The phrase "in a house" modifies the verb "lives.")

He is a man *of* principles.
("Of" is the preposition. "Of principles" modifies the noun "man.")

In Greek, each preposition requires a certain grammatical case. That is, the noun after the preposition must appear in the appropriate form, according to the preposition. Some prepositions can use more than one case, and the preposition can have a different meaning with each differing case.

ἐν (*en*, "in" or "on") used with the dative case, indicates location.

ὁ ἄνθρωπος ἐστὶν ἐν τῇ γῇ.
(*ho án<u>th</u>rōpos estín en tē gē.*)
The man is on (or in) the earth.

ἐκ (*ek*, "from," "of") used with the genitive case, indicates movement away from something.

ὁ κύριος ἐξῆλθον ἐκ τῆς γῆς.
(*ho kúrios exē'l<u>th</u>on ek tēs gēs.*)
The Lord went from the earth.

εἰς (*eis*, "in," "toward") used with the accusative case, indicates movement toward something.

ὁ κύριος ἔρχει εἰς τὸν οὐρανόν.
(*ho kúrios ér<u>ch</u>ei eis ton <u>u</u>ranón.*)

The Lord goes to heaven.

περί (*perí*) means "about" or "concerning" when it is used with the genitive case, and "around" when it is used with the accusative case.

λαλοῦμεν περὶ τοῦ λόγου.
(*lalúmen perí tu lógu.*)
We talk about the word.

ἔρχομαι περὶ τὴν γῆν.
(*érchomai perí tēn gēn.*)
I go around the earth.

πρός (pros) means "toward" when used with the accusative case (as is most common in the New Testament), but it can mean "to the advantage of," or "to be essential to," when used with the genitive case, and "near" or "before" when used with the dative case (uses more common in other Greek literature outside the NT). *This is why Robertson mentions the accusative case in his commentary on John 1:1.* He says it presents a "plane of equality and intimacy, face to face with each other."

You will have to observe which case is required by each preposition when you learn the vocabulary, or when you look up the word in a dictionary.

Vocabulary List #3, Part B

Observe the following list and drawing[25] to distinguish the meaning of some important prepositions. Some of these words use several cases and have several different meanings, but for now we will show only the meanings related to movement or location. Memorize the prepositions and their meanings. You can practice with the PowerPoint exercises on *Thirdmill* or *LaBibliaaFondo.* (See the Preface for the addresses.) Click on "06 Vocabulary List #3b".

περί	(*perí*) around (with accus.)
ὑπέρ	(*hupér*) over (with accus.)
ἐπί	(*epí*) on (with genitive)
πρός	(*pros*) toward (with accus.)
εἰς	(*eis*) into (with accus.)
ἐν	(*en*) in (with dative)
ἐκ	(*ek*) out of (with genitive)
ἀπό	(*apó*) from (with genitive)
διά	(*diá*) through (with genitive)
ὑπό	(*hupó*) under (with accus.)

---

[25] The graphic is based on one by Bruce M. Metzger, *Lexical Aids for Students of New Testament Greek*, p. 80.

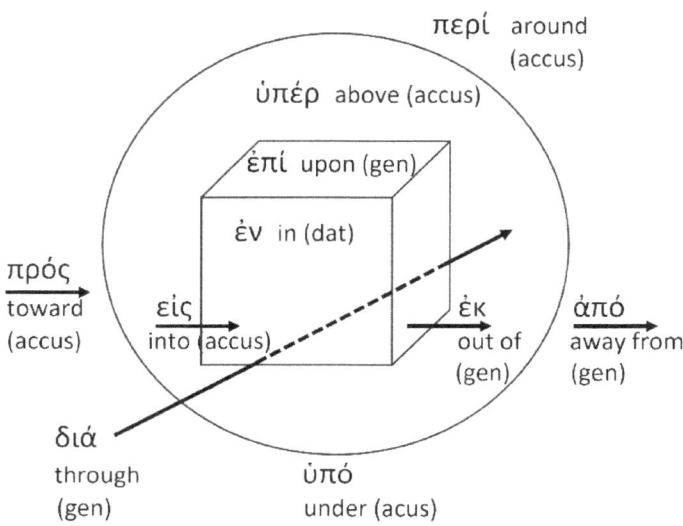

7.5. Romans 1:17

Prepositions can sometimes be tricky little words. To translate them properly, it's really important to consider the context and to search for other passages that use the words in a similar way. For example, Romans 1:17 is difficult to understand in some translations.

For therein is the righteousness of God revealed from faith to faith: as it is written, the just shall live by faith. (King James)

For in it the righteousness of God is revealed from faith to faith; as it is written, "But the righteous man shall live by faith." (New American Standard)

What does the phrase "from faith to faith" mean? At first it sounds nice, but when you think about it, you are not sure what it means. Is it talking about different kinds of faith, or about passing the faith from one person to another? There are some loose translations that give totally different interpretations.

The good news tells how God accepts everyone who has faith, but only those who have faith. It is just as the Scriptures say, "The people God accepts because of their faith will live." (Contemporary English Version)

God's way of putting people right shows up in the acts of faith, confirming what Scripture has said all along: "The person in right standing before God by trusting him really lives." (The Message)

When we look at the Greek text, we find it very helpful. The phrase is ἐκ πίστεως εἰς πίστιν (*ek písteōs eis pístin*). The word ἐκ (*ek*) is a preposition that is often used to describe movement from inside to outside, for example to explain that someone went *out of* a house. On the other hand, the word εἰς (*eis*) is a preposition that is often used to describe movement from the outside in, for example to explain that someone went *into* a house.

Greek and Exegesis

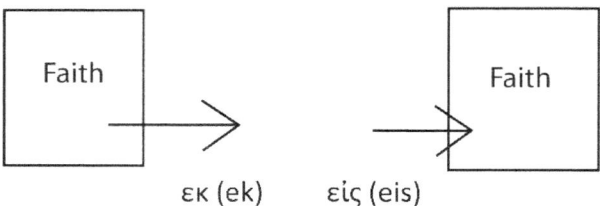

εκ (ek)   εἰς (eis)

The phrase awakens an image of a journey that begins in an area of faith and ends in another area of faith. While it is not exactly a literal translation of this verse, the *New International Version* communicates the idea:

For in the gospel a righteousness of God is revealed, a righteousness that is by faith from first to last.

The *New Living Translation*, even less literal, shares the interpretation:

This Good News tells us how God makes us right in his sight. This is accomplished from start to finish by faith.

The context of the letter to the Romans supports these two translations. This verse is an introduction to the whole epistle, in which Paul deals especially with the themes of justification and sanctification. Verse 17 is announcing that righteousness comes from God, that it is received initially by faith (in justification), and that it continues to be nourished by faith (in sanctification) throughout life until the end. In other words, justification (righteousness in terms of our legal standing) is by faith, and sanctification (righteousness in terms of our personal walk in holiness) is also by faith, even until we are glorified in the presence of Christ! There is no righteousness that does not come from God by faith.

7.6. Acts 2:38

In Acts 2:38, Peter says "repent and be baptized...*for* the forgiveness of your sins." (ESV) Some people take this to mean that the sacrament itself produces forgiveness, or even that you must be baptized to be saved. However, this would contradict many other key passages in the New Testament that teach salvation by grace through faith alone (Romans 1:16-17, Romans 3:28, Ephesians 2:8-10, for example).

The word in Acts 2:38 translated "for" is εἰς ("eis") in Greek, which can mean "into," "in," "unto," "to," "towards," "for," "on", or "among." It helps to see that the same Greek word εἰς is used in a similar context in Romans 6:4, "We were buried therefore with him by baptism *into* death,..." (ESV). Obviously, this verse does not mean that baptism produces death! It's even more clear when you look at the parallel verse in Romans 6:3, where it says "baptized into *his* death" (εἰς τὸν θάνατον αὐτοῦ), referring to Jesus. I would suggest that in Acts 2:38 and Romans 6:3 and 4, the phrases tell us what baptism *represents*. Baptism is "for" forgiveness in the sense that it represents forgiveness, and it is "into" death in the sense that it represents our spiritual death (and resurrection) with Christ.

In *Logos*, E4's Greek Lexicon (E4GL) says the following about the word εἰς in Acts 2:38:

> "For" (as used in Ac 2:38 "for the forgiveness...") could have two meanings. If you saw a poster saying "Jesse James wanted for robbery", "for" could mean

Jesse is wanted so he can commit a robbery, or is wanted because he has committed a robbery. The later sense is the correct one. So too in this passage, the word "for" signifies an action in the past. Otherwise, it would violate the entire tenor of the NT teaching on salvation by grace and not by works.[26]

EXERCISES

Before doing these exercises, you can practice with the PowerPoint exercises on *Thirdmill* or *LaBibliaaFondo.* (See the Preface for the addresses.) Click on "07 Other Parts of Speech".

a. Identify all the adjectives, adverbs, pronouns, and prepositions in the following sentences, both English and Greek. Write "ADJ" below the adjectives, "ADV" below the adverbs, "Pron" below pronouns, and "Prep" below the prepositions. Also, translate the Greek sentences into English. For the sentences in Greek, make sure you identify the adjectives, adverbs, pronouns and prepositions in Greek, which may or may not coincide with the adjectives, adverbs, pronouns and prepositions in the English translation. Note what noun or pronoun is modified by each adjective and what verb is modified by each adverb.

1) The tall man often bought good books in the bookstore.

---

[26] *E4's Greek Dictionary* (electronic ed., 2001). Ephesians Four Group (In *Logos* software).

2) He went gladly from the city to the beautiful mountains with her.

3) ὁ ἀνὴρ ὁ ἅγιος λέγει νῦν ἐν τῇ γῇ.

4) ἡ γυνὴ ἡ ἅγια ἔρχεται νῦν εἰς τὸν κύριον ἡμῶν. (ἔρχεται means "comes.")

5) δίδωμι οὕτως αὐτῇ τὸν λόγον τὸν ἅγιον.

b. Make a brief list of any adjectives, adverbs, pronouns or prepositions that are important for understanding John 3:16. Make some notes about why they are important.

EXEGESIS ASSIGNMENT #5: OTHER PARTS OF SPEECH

Logos

The steps for finding the form of Greek adjectives, adverbs, pronouns, and prepositions in *Logos* software are the same as for nouns:

1. Find your study passage in the Greek New Testament.
2. Open the "Exegetical guide" and find the list of words in each verse "Word by Word."
3. Scroll down to the word you want to analyze.
4. It gives you the root form and several definitions.
5. You can listen to the pronunciation of the word.
6. You can look again at dictionary meanings by clicking on any of the dictionaries listed.
7. You can also read the explanation of the form.
8. Identify all the adjectives, adverbs, pronouns, and prepositions in your passage.

e-Sword

1. Open the New Testament version "Greek NT WH+".
2. Find any word you want to analyze and pass the pointer over the code above it to the right. It will open a window with the basic information.
3. Identify all the adjectives, adverbs, pronouns, and prepositions in your passage.

For the "Exegesis Report":

1. Copy your passage in Greek and write "ADJ" below the adjectives, "ADV" below the adverbs, "Pron" below pronouns, and "Prep" below the prepositions.

2. Indicate what noun or pronoun is modified by each adjective and indicate what verb is modified by each adverb.

3. Make a brief list of any adjectives, adverbs, pronouns or prepositions that are important for understanding your passage. Make some notes about why they are important.

8. VERBS, PART 1

In this lesson, you will learn the principal forms of the Greek verb. When you finish, you will be able to explain the meaning of the Greek tenses and you will be able to translate verbs according to their tense, person, and number.

Verbs are the principal part of a sentence. A verb describes the action or the condition of the subject. As well as being the most important part of the sentence, the verb also the most complex aspect. The Greek verb has tenses, voices, and moods, as well as person and number.

The study of just one verb can change our interpretation of a text, or it might even affect our theology. For example, in the NASB95 translation, 1 John 3:6 and 9 say,

No one who abides in Him sins; no one who sins has seen Him or knows Him. (6)

No one who is born of God practices sin, because His seed abides in him; and he cannot sin, because he is born of God. (9)

Does this mean that a Christian never sins? Other Bible passages, even within the same letter of John, indicate that a Christian still commits sin and can be forgiven. Do these verses contradict the other passages? A study of the verbs will help us interpret these verses. We will explain this later. First, you need to learn some new vocabulary:

Vocabulary List #4

Learn this list of words. Learn to pronounce them and memorize their meanings. You can practice with the PowerPoint exercises on *Thirdmill* or *LaBibliaaFondo.* (See the Preface for the addresses.) Click on "08 Vocabulary List #4".

ἀποστέλλω	(*apostélō*) I send [an apostle is a "sent one"]
θέλω	(*thélō*) I desire
καλέω	(*kaléō*) I call, I invite
λαμβάνω	(*lambánō*) I take, I receive
λύω	(*lúō*) I loose, I free
μετά	(*metá*) with (used with gen.), after (used with accus.)[27]
οὖν	(*un*) then
πατήρ	(*patē´r*) father [*pater*nal]
πίστις	(*pístis*) faith, belief
πνεῦμα	(*néuma*)[28] spirit
πολύς, πολλή, πολύ	(*polús*) much, many [*poly*theism, *poly*gamy]

---

[27] The philosophical term "metaphysics" has its origin in the fact that in Aristotle's writings, the study of being came *after* the study of *physics*.

[28] Remember that the combination of letters pn is pronounced like an "n."

| σῶμα | (sō´ma) body [psychosomatic, sickness of the body related to psychological factors] |
| φωνή | (phonē´) voice [phonetics] |

8.1. Tenses

In English, there are the following verb tenses:

TENSE	EXAMPLE
Simple	
Present	I look
Past	I looked
Future	I will look
Progressive	
Present progressive	I am looking
Past progressive	I was looking
Future progressive	I shall (or will) be looking
Perfect	
Present perfect	I have looked
Past perfect	I had looked
Future perfect	I shall (or will) have looked

Notice that a verb tense includes two elements: aspect and time. The aspect can be simple, progressive, or perfect. Simple is like a snapshot, progressive is ongoing like a movie, and perfect is a completed action, like a book that has been closed.[29]

In Greek, there are similar tenses, but some of the names are changed. Instead of "past progressive," Greek has the "imperfect" tense. Instead of "past perfect," Greek has "pluperfect." Instead of "past," Greek has "aorist." Greek does have a future perfect, but it is only used a few times in the New Testament, so it will not be studied in this course. The Greek present tense is used for both concepts of simple present and present progressive.

We should explain that the Greek *aorist* is not exactly the same as the English *past*. In some moods, it may not necessarily indicate much about time, or action in the past. It definitely does not indicate past progressive, because the imperfect fulfills that function. Some have described the aorist as being punctiliar. However, probably the best way to summarize its meaning is to say it describes an action *in its totality*. This will be discussed more completely in the next lesson.

At the risk of over-simplifying, we will show the parallel Greek terms for the verb tenses.

---

[29] Some linguists consider the *aspect* more important than the *time* in Greek verbs. See Seumas Macdonald, "The New understandings in Greek, Part 1: Verbs, Aspect and Tense," <https://thepatrologist.com/2015/09/22/the-new-understandings-in-greek-part-1-verbs-aspect-and-tense/>.

ENGLISH TENSE	EXAMPLE	GREEK TENSE
Simple		
Present	I look	Present
Past	I looked	Aorist
Future	I will look	Future
Progressive		
Present progressive	I am looking	Present
Past progressive	I was looking	Imperfect
Future progressive	I shall be looking	
Perfect		
Present perfect	I have looked	Perfect
Past perfect	I had looked	Pluperfect
Future perfect	I shall have looked	*

   * Future Perfect will not be studied in this course, since it occurs infrequently in the N.T.

   We could symbolize the meaning of the Greek tenses the following way. The capital A symbolizes an action, a dotted line (-------) indicates continued action, and the > or < indicates the point of view of the speaker. Notice that we will begin to change the order of the tenses as we list them, since Greek grammars usually follow this pattern:

Present

Either "I look," or   A

simple action in the present, or

"I am looking"   - - - - - - - - -

progressive action at present time

Imperfect

"I was looking"   - - - - - - - <

continuous action in the past

Future

"I will look"   >   A

a future action, anticipated now

Aorist

"I looked"   [A]

action seen in its totality

(sometimes, not always, in the past)

Perfect

"I have looked"   A ⟶ <

action (A) *completed* in the past,

whose effects continue now

Pluperfect

"I had looked"   A1   A2   <

past action (A1) previous to another

past action (A2)

8.2. Matthew 4:17

Notice the importance of observing differences in verb tenses for interpreting Matthew 4:17. This verse gives a summary of Jesus' preaching, which is translated in the ESV as "Repent, for the kingdom of heaven *is at hand.*" John the Baptist is recorded in Matthew 3:2 as preaching the same thing. See the following different translations of the last phrase:

The ESV: "...the kingdom of heaven is at hand."
The NIV84: "...the kingdom of heaven is near."
A later NIV version: "...the kingdom of heaven has come near."
The *Contemporary English Version:* "...the kingdom of heaven will soon be here."
The Message: "...God's kingdom is here."
The New Revised Standard Version: "...the kingdom of heaven has come near."

Which is the best translation? What does the phrase mean? The *Contemporary English Version* ("...will soon be here") could give the impression that they were still waiting for the kingdom to come. The NIV84 could also be understood that way ("...the kingdom of heaven is near.") The Greek verb in the last phrase is ἤγγικεν (to come near or be near) and it is in *the perfect tense.* As we have seen, the perfect tense indicates an *action completed in the past whose effects continue now.* That means *something already happened.* The difference between "is near" and "has come near" is that the second phrase indicates *movement* has already occurred. It's like the difference between saying the hospital "is near" and the ambulance "has come near." The same verb ἤγγικεν is used in Matthew 26:46 when Jesus says, "My betrayer is at hand" (ESV). We see in the next verse that Judas was already arriving when Jesus spoke these words. ("While he was still speaking, Judas came.") The theme of the coming of the kingdom is complicated because it comes in stages (See Acts 1:6), but we know that with the coming of Jesus there was a radical change in the development of the kingdom: the King had arrived! It seems that the best translation is "...the kingdom of heaven *has come near*." As the New Bible Commentary says, Jesus was proclaiming in Matthew 4:17 that "God is king, and his rule was now being made effective." [30]

8.3. Person and Number

You may remember from English grammar that verbs have person and number. First person is "I" or "we," second person is "you" singular or plural, and third person is "he, she, it, or they." Look at the different forms of the verb "loose" in English in the present tense.

1 sing	I loose
2 sing	you loose
3 sing	he, she, or it looses
1 plural	we loose

---

[30] R.T. France, in Matthew, D. A. Carson, R. T. France, J. A. Motyer, & G. J. Wenham (eds.), *New Bible commentary: 21st century edition* (4th ed., 1994, p. 910). Inter-Varsity Press. (In Logos software.)

2 plural	you (pl) loose
3 plural	they loose

The verb for "loose" in Greek is λύω. The following table shows the *present tense*.

Memorize these forms:

1 s	λύω	I loose
2 s	λύεις	you loose
3 s	λύει	he, she, or it looses
1 pl	λύομεν	we loose
2 pl	λύετε	you (pl) loose
3 pl	λύουσι[ν]	they loose

Notice the final letters. You can have a good idea of the person and the number of the verb by observing these endings.

1 s	-ω, -α, -ον
2 s	-ς
3 s	-ει, -ε, -εν
1 pl	-μεν
2 pl	-τε
3 pl	-σι(ν), -σαν, -ον

8.4 Guidelines for Recognizing Verb Tenses

Traditionally, students of Greek had to learn to identify verb tenses without the help of linguistic programs. Now we have programs like *e-Sword* and *Logos* that indicate information about the verbs. However, it is good to memorize a few forms and know some basic things so that you are not always completely dependent on such tools. We offer the following guidelines:

Memorize these forms of λύω in 1st person singular, all tenses:

Pres	Impf	Fut	Aor	Perf	Plupf
λύω	ἔλυον	λύσω	ἔλυσα	λέλυκα	ἐλελύκειν
I loose	I was loosing	I shall loose	I loosed	I have loosed	I had loosed

Notice the changes:

a. Imperfect adds an ε at the beginning. (Sometimes the vowel is changed for a long vowel, for example if the word begins with ε, it is changed to a η.)

b. Future adds a σ at the end of the root.

c. Aorist adds both a ε at the beginning and a σ after the root.

d. Perfect adds a reduplication of the sound of the first letter (λε-, in this case), plus a κ after the root.

e. Pluperfect adds the ε, then the reduplication (λε-, in this case), plus the κ after the root.

The following table summarizes the pattern. V represents the main verb root (λύ), and R represents a reduplication. The clues to the verb tense are highlighted in **bold**.

V	= present	λύω	I loose
ε V	= imperfect	ἔλυον	I was loosing
V σ	= future	λύσω	I shall loose
ε V σ	= aorist	ἔλυσα	I loosed
RV κ	= perfect	λέλυκα	I have loosed
ε RV κ	= pluperfect	ἐλελύκειν	I had loosed

The following table is another way of summarizing these guidelines for recognizing the tenses in indicative mood. Look at each tense in the top row, then notice the signs for each one as you read down the column.

Key for Recognizing Greek Verb Tenses

	Pres	Imp	Fut	Aor	Perf	Plupf
Augment		ε		ε		ε
Reduplication					R	R
Addition to the root			σ	σ	κ	κ

The important thing is to know what the tenses mean and how they should be translated. At the end of this chapter you can see the full table of the forms of the verb λύω in the indicative mood. (We will study the meaning of the moods later.) This table is called the *paradigm* or the *conjugation* of the verb. Sometimes students are required to memorize all the forms of λύω. We make the table available for those who would like to become proficient in reading Greek without so much help from linguistic software.

8.5. Irregular Verbs

English has many irregular verbs. The *regular* way to form a past tense is to add "–ed" to the end of the present tense. For example, "jump" becomes "jumped." However, the irregular verbs do not follow this pattern. For instance, "run" becomes "ran," "swim" becomes "swam," and "win" becomes "won." Unfortunately, the verbs used most tend to be irregular.

The same is true for Greek. One important irregular verb is εἰμί, "I am". Notice the conjugation in the following table:

	Present	Imperfect	Future
1 s.	εἰμί	ἤμην	ἔσομαι
	I am	I was	I will be
2 s.	εἶ	ἦς	ἔσῃ
	You are	You were	You will be
3 s.	ἐστί[ν]	ἦν	ἔσται
	He or she is	He or she was	He or she will be
1 pl.	ἐσμέν	ἦμεν	ἐσόμεθα
	We are	We were	We will be
2 pl.	ἐστέ	ἦτε	ἔσεσθε
	You (pl) are	You (pl) were	You (pl) will be
3 pl.	εἰσί	ἦσαν	ἔσονται
	They are	They were	They will be

There are many irregular forms. The important thing for now is to *know that they exist*. When you look up the root form of a verb, you might be surprised at how different it is from the word you are analyzing in a New Testament verse. You might think there is a mistake, unless you realize that it is an irregular verb. Some Greek verbs have an aorist form that is very different from the root form, and do not follow the regular pattern. This is called the "second aorist."

119

EXERCISES

First, practice with the PowerPoint exercises on *Thirdmill* or *LaBibliaaFondo.* (See the Preface for the addresses.) Click on "09 Verbs, Part 1". We recommend that you print the pages with these exercises and write the answers by hand.

a. Describe the meaning of each verb tense in Greek:

present

imperfect

future

aorist

perfect

pluperfect

b. Identify the verb tense according to the pattern. V represents the main verb root, and R represents a reduplication.

    T
  ε T
    T σ
  ε T σ
  RT κ
  ε RT κ

c. Write the forms of the present indicative of λύω.

1 sing	
2 sing	
3 sing	
1 plural	
2 plural	
3 plural	

d. Write the Greek forms of λύω in 1st person singular, all tenses:

Pres	Impf	Fut	Aor	Perf	Plupf
--------	--------	--------	--------	--------	--------
I loose	I was loosing	I shall loose	I loosed	I have loosed	I had loosed

e. Observe the tense, person, and number of the following verbs, and translate them.

	Tense	Person	Num	Translation
λύω	Pres	1	S	
λύει	Pres	3	S	
λύομεν	Pres	1	Pl	
λύουσι	Pres	3	Pl	
ἐλύομεν	Impf	1	Pl	
ἐλύετε	Impf	2	Pl	
λύσει	Fut	3	S	
λύσουσιν	Fut	3	Pl	
ἔλυσας	Aor	2	S	
ἐλύσαμεν	Aor	1	Pl	
λέλυκα	Perf	1	S	
ἐλελύκεισαν	Plupf	3	Pl	

e. Practice the vocabulary with the PowerPoint exercises on *Thirdmill* or *LaBibliaaFondo.* (See the Preface for the addresses.) Click on "08 Vocabulary List #4".

The Conjugation of λύω in the Indicative Mood

Below is the full table of the forms of the verb λύω (*lúō,* I free, or I loose) in all the verb tenses in indicative mood. (We will study the meaning and forms of the other moods later.) This paradigm is called the *conjugation* or *paradigm* of the verb.

Notice that some verbs have a second form with an (ν) in parentheses. This is sometimes used when the following word begins with a vowel, or when the verb comes at the end of a sentence. For example, we may find λύουσιν ἐκ... We assume this change was to make the pronunciation easier.

Observe the forms. It's not necessary to memorize all of them, but we recommend that you at least learn the forms of the present tense and all tenses in first person singular (all the highlighted words).

Paradigm of the regular verb, λύω (indicative mood)

Singular

	Pres	Imperf	Fut	Aor	Perf	Plpf
1	λύω — I loose	ἔλυον — I was loosing	λύσω — I shall loose	ἔλυσα — I loosed	λέλυκα — I have loosed	ἐλελύκειν — I had loosed
2	λύεις — you loose	ἔλυες — you were loosing	λύσεις — you shall loose	ἔλυσας — You loosed	λέλυκας — You have loosed	ἐλελύκεις — You had loosed
3	λύει — he, she looses	ἔλυε[ν] — he, she was loosing	λύσει — he, she shall loose	ἔλυσε[ν] — He, she loosed	λέλυκε[ν] — He, she has loosed	ἐλελύκει — He, she had loosed

Plural

	Pres	Imperf	Fut	Aor	Perf	Plpf
1	λύομεν We loose	ἐλύομεν We were loosing	λύσομεν We shall loose	ἐλύσαμεν We loosed	λελύκαμεν We have loosed	ἐλελύκειμεν We had loosed
2	λύετε You loose	ἐλύετε You were loosing	λύσετε You shall loose	ἐλύσατε You loosed	λελύκατε You have loosed	ἐλελύκειτε You had loosed
3	λύουσι[ν] They loose	ἔλυον They were loosing	λύσουσι[ν] They shall loose	ἔλυσαν They loosed	λελύκασι[ν] They have loosed	ἐλελύκεισαν They had loosed

9. Verbs, Part 2

In this lesson you will learn about moods, voices, deponent verbs, and the use of participles. When you finish the lesson, you will be able to explain the meaning of the different moods and voices in Greek. You will also be able to use the information about verbs to translate them into English.

First, learn a new list of vocabulary:

Vocabulary List #5

Learn this list of words. Learn to pronounce them and memorize their meanings. You can practice with the PowerPoint exercises on *Thirdmill* or *LaBibliaaFondo*. (See the Preface for the addresses.) Click on "10 Vocabulary List #5".

ἄγγελος	(*ángelos*) messenger, angel
ἁμαρτία	(*hamartía*) sin
βασιλεία	(*basileia*) kingdom [basilica, originally a king's palace]
γίνομαι	(*gínomai*) I become
γράφω	(*gráphō*) I write [*graph*ics, calligraphy]
δόξα	(*dóxa*) glory [*dox*ology]

ἔθνος	(éthnos) nation, ethnic group, gentile
ἔργον	(érgon) work [synergy]
ἐσθίω	(esthíō) I eat
εὑρίσκω	(heurískō) find [eureka!]
ἵστημι	(hístēmi) I stand
καθώς	(kathō's) as, just as
καρδία	(kardía) heart [cardiology]

9.1. Active and Passive Voices

In English, verbs can be either in *active voice* or *passive voice*. Active voice is used when the subject acts. The passive voice is used when the subject receives the action passively. For example, in the sentence using active voice, "The man bought a book," "the man" is the subject, "bought" is the verb in active voice, and "book" is the direct object.

  The man ‖ bought |--> a book

But we can express the same idea using passive voice: "The book was bought by the man."

  The book ‖ was bought
              \ by the man

In this case, "the book" is the subject that receives the action of the verb "was bought."

128

Greek verbs can also be in active or passive voice, but there is also a third voice called middle voice. The middle voice expresses the idea that the subject is indirectly affected by the action or that the subject acted upon himself. It is translated to English with expressions such as "for himself" or "for herself." ("The man bought a book for himself.") Interestingly, in Greek, these concepts of active, passive and middle voice are expressed completely within the verb itself.

For example:

ἔλυσα	(élusa) "I loosed" (active voice)
ἐλύθην	(elúthēn) "I was loosed" (passive voice)
ἐλυσάμην	(elusámēn) "I loosed myself" or "I loosed something for myself." (middle voice)

In most tenses (all but aorist and future) the form of the middle voice and the form of the passive voice are the same. Only the context will indicate which one it is. For example, λύομαι (lúomai) can be taken as passive voice (I am loosed) or as middle voice (I loose for myself).

The following table compares the present active and the present middle/passive forms of λύω.

Present Tense Active Voice	Present Tense Middle/Passive Voice
λύω I loose	λύω I loose myself/ I am loosed
λύεις You loose	λύῃ you loose yourself/ you are loosed
λύει He, she looses	λύεται he, she looses himself, herself/ he, she is loosed
λύομεν We loose	λυόμεθα we loose ourselves/ we are loosed
λύετε You loose	λύεσθε you loose yourselves/ you are loosed
λύουσι[ν] They loose	λύονται they loose themselves/ they are loosed

Notice the frequent use of αι and θ in the middle/passive forms.

9.2. Deponent Verbs

Some verbs use the *form* of middle or passive voice with the *meaning* of active voice. This is a kind of irregularity, and they are called "deponent" verbs. You need to be careful in translating these verbs, because you might think they have the meaning of middle or passive voice (the subject acting upon himself or being acted upon), but they should be translated simply as active voice.

For example:

ἔρχομαι (érchomai, "I come") is a deponent verb in present tense and in future tense (λεύσομαι, eléusomai, "I shall come"). It has the form of middle voice, but the meaning of active voice.

γίνομαι (gínomai, "I become") is also deponent in present and future (γενήσομαι genē'somai, "I shall become").

εἰμί (eimí, I am) is defective in the future tense (ἔσομαι, ésomai, I shall be).

How can you know if a verb is deponent? You can look up the word in a dictionary that shows the principal parts. For example, in the *Concise Greek-English Dictionary of the NT* (ed. Barclay M. Newman), the verb εἰμί indicates that the future form is ἔσομαι. From the ending -μαι, you know that it is deponent in future. Linguistic software such as *Logos* and *e-Sword* can help you identify deponent verbs.

9.3. Moods

In addition to tense, person, number, and voice, verbs are also classified by *mood*. In Greek, there are the following moods: indicative, subjunctive, imperative, infinitive, and participle.

131

Mood	Meaning	Grk	Eng
Indicative	Indicates something	λύει	He or she looses
Subjunctive	Shows probability, purpose, emotion, contrary to reality	λύῃ	He or she might loose
Imperative	Command	λῦε	Loose!
		λυέτω	May he or she loose!
Infinitive	Unlimited (Can be use as a noun)	λύειν	To loose
Participle	Combines characteristics of verb and adjective	λύων	Loosing

A participle is a verb form used as an adjective, as in "The *talking* bird surprised us." Note that in Greek, the imperative may also be in third person, λυέτω (*luétō*) "May he loose." The following sentences show the difference in the moods.

Indicative
ὁ ἄνθρωπος **λύει** τὸν δοῦλον.
(*ho ánthrōpos lúei ton dulon*.)
The man **frees** the slave.

Subjunctive
ἔρχομαι ἵνα ὁ ἄνθρωπος **λύῃ** τὸν δοῦλον.
(*érchomai hína ho ánthrōpos lúē ton dúlon.*)
I come so that the man **might free** the slave.

Imperative
λῦε τὸν δοῦλον.
(*lúe ton dúlon.*)
Free the slave!

Infinitive
θέλω **λύειν** τὸν δοῦλον.
(*thélō lúein ton dúlon.*)
I desire **to free** the slave.

Participle
λύων τὸν δοῦλον, ὁ ἄνθρωπος βλέπει τὸν ἀδελφὸν.
(*lúōn ton dúlon, ho ánthrōpos blépei ton adelphón su.*)
Freeing the slave, the man sees the brother.

There is another mood called the "optative" mood, which is not used very often in the New Testament. It expresses a wish. Paul sometimes uses it to express a negative wish, such as in Romans 6:2, μὴ γένοιτο, "may it not be!" or "By no means!" (ESV).

Observe the forms of the different moods of λύω in present tense, active voice:

Indicative

1 s	λύω	I free
2 s	λύεις	you free
3 s	λύει	he or she frees
1 pl	λύομεν	we free
2 pl	λύετε	you (pl) free
3 pl	λύουσι[ν]	they free

Subjunctive

1 s	λύω	I might free
2 s	λύῃ	you might free
3 s	λύῃ	he, she might free
1 pl	λύωμεν	we might free
2 pl	λύητε	you might free
3 pl	λύωσι[ν]	they might free

Imperative

2 s	λῦε	Free!
3 s	λυέτω	May he, she free!
2 pl	λύετε	Free!
3 pl	λυέτωσαν	May they free!

Infinitive

λύειν   to free

Participle

λύων   freeing

9.4. The Meaning of the Aorist Tense

Now that we have reviewed the verb moods, we need to explain a little more about the meaning of the aorist tense. The temptation is to always consider it the equivalent of past tense in English. However, even though the aorist usually does refer to past tense in the indicative mood, in other moods it does not put the emphasis on the time or duration of the action. In general, the aorist expresses an action in its totality, simply as something that happens.

Linguists emphasize the general meaning of aorist as limitless. The Greek word ἀόριστος means "indefinite" or "without boundaries." Richard Young explains that the difference between the present tense and the aorist tense in Greek is like the difference between observing a parade from the side of the street and observing the same parade from a helicopter. The present tense watches each participant as they pass by, while the aorist watches the event in its totality.[31]

---

[31] Richard Young, *Intermediate New Testament Greek* (Nashville, Tennessee: Broadman and Holman, 1994), p. 122.

Greek and Exegesis

Experts suggest that the aorist is the most important of Greek tenses, and that it is the "most characteristic of the Greek language." Dana and Mantey explain that "The fundamental meaning of the aorist is to denote action simply as occurring, without reference to its progress... It has no special temporal significance, finding its time relationships only in the Indicative where it is used as past tense." They say that the aorist "establishes the fact of the action or event, without consideration of its duration," and that it "denotes an action simply as an event, without defining in any way the manner of its occurrence."[32]

The difference between λυέτω (luétō, present Imperative, third person singular, active voice) and λυσάτω (lusátō, aorist Imperative, third person singular, active voice) is that the present suggests progression, while the aorist suggests something more indefinite. Since it is difficult to communicate the difference in English, the translations may be the same, or they might be different. The context will determine the meaning.

λυέτω
   May he or she free...!
   May he or she continue freeing....!

λυσάτω
   May he or she free!
   May he or she begin to free!

---

[32] H. E. Dana and Julius R. Mantey, *Gramática griega del Nuevo Testamento* (El Paso: Casa Bautista, 1975), p. 186-187.

9.5. The Use of the Participle

Since participles are very common in the New Testament, you need to know some typical ways they are used. As previously stated, the participle combines characteristics of a verb (tense and voice) and characteristics of an adjective (gender, number and case). These attributes allow for flexibility and variety in its role in the sentence.

In general, you can initially translate them with the verb ending in "-ing" (for example, "believing"), then consider the context to determine the precise meaning and the best way to translate it. If the participle is in aorist tense, you might initially translate it, "having" + the verb (e.g. "having believed").

As an adjective

Sometimes participles are used as adjectives. For example, Matthew 3:17 says, "And behold, a voice from heaven said..." (ESV). In Greek, it is:

καὶ ἰδοὺ φωνὴ ἐκ τῶν οὐρανῶν λέγουσα

The participle λέγουσα (from "say") modifies the noun φωνὴ (voice). It says literally, "And behold, a voice from heaven saying,..."

As an adverbial phrase

More often, the participle is used as an adverbial phrase, a phrase that modifies another verb. Matthew 26:26 provides an example. Part of the verse says, "...after taking bread and blessing it, Jesus broke it..." (ESV). In Greek it is:

λαβὼν ὁ Ἰησοῦς ἄρτον καὶ εὐλογήσας ἔκλασεν

This phrase contains two participles, both in aorist tense: λαβὼν (to take) and εὐλογήσας (to bless or give thanks). The main verb is ἔκλασεν (to break), in aorist tense, indicative mood. This could be translated literally "having taken Jesus bread and having given thanks, he broke (it)". Both participles function as adverbs, because they explain when Jesus broke the bread.

The Genitive Absolute

Another frequent use of the participle in the Greek New Testament is called the "genitive absolute." It's a phrase with a participle in the *genitive* case, which doesn't combine grammatically with the rest of the sentence in the usual way. It is "absolute" in the sense that it is independent; the phrase sort of stands separately by itself. The participle is often combined with a noun or pronoun also in *genitive* case, which serves as the subject of the participle.

The first phrase of the same verse, Matthew 26:26, provides an example. It is translated, "Now as they were eating,…" In Greek it says,

Ἐσθιόντων δὲ αὐτῶν

The first word is a participle in present tense, Ἐσθιόντων (literally "eating"), and αὐτῶν is a pronoun in third person plural, genitive case (normally translated "of them" or "their"). If we don't realize that this is a genitive absolute, we might

138

begin with a literal translation, which would be something like this: "And eating of them." But that doesn't make sense. If we remember how a genitive absolute functions, we realize that "they" is the subject of "eating." Literally it says, "And eating, they…" For translating genitive absolutes, William Mounce recommends that we start by adding the word "while" if the participle is in present tense, and "after" if the participle is in aorist tense.[33] If we follow that guideline, a good translation of this phrase would be "While they were eating,…"

9.6. 1 John 3:6
The significance of the participle might help us analyze passages such as 1 John 3:6.

> 1 John 3:6 (NASB95)
> No one who abides in Him sins; no one who sins has seen Him or knows Him.
>
> πᾶς ὁ ἐν αὐτῷ μένων οὐχ ἁμαρτάνει· πᾶς ὁ ἁμαρτάνων οὐχ ἑώρακεν αὐτὸν οὐδὲ ἔγνωκεν αὐτόν.

At first sight, the first phrase, "No one who abides in Him sins," appears to contradict other Biblical passages, including these verses in chapter one of the same letter.

---

[33] William Mounce, *Basics of Biblical Greek* (Grand Rapids: Zondervan, 1993), p. 275.

Greek and Exegesis

1 John 1:8-9 (NASB95)
If we say that we have no sin, we are deceiving ourselves and the truth is not in us. If we confess our sins, He is faithful and righteous to forgive us our sins and to cleanse us from all unrighteousness.

Our study of participles can help us find a solution. One possible interpretation is that John is saying, *while one is abiding in Christ*, as a branch abides in the vine, he will not sin. That is, when we are trusting Christ, living by faith, with our eyes on Him, we can resist temptation. This doesn't mean we will constantly maintain that strong faith and a close relationship with the Lord, and if we do sin, it doesn't mean we have lost our salvation, or that we were never saved; it means we need to confess our sin and ask for the Lord's help. The fact that the word "abides" is a participle (μένων), which means literally, "abiding", may lend support to this view.[34]

Another possible interpretation is that John is saying, those who truly believe in Christ will not continue living a life characterized by sin.[35] Those who hold this view can appeal to the fact that the first phrase of the verse is parallel to the second phrase, expressing the same thought. Notice the second phrase, "no one who sins has seen him...", uses a present tense particle (ἁμαρτάνων), suggesting continued action. It says literally, "everyone who *is sinning* has not seen him..." Several translations support this interpretation:

---

[34] See the commentary of Jamieson, Fausset and Brown.
[35] Morris, L. L., "1 John", in the *New Bible commentary: 21st century edition* (4th ed., p. 1404). Inter-Varsity Press, 1994.

The ESV translates verse 3:6 as:

No one who abides in him *keeps on sinning*; no one who *keeps on sinning* has either seen him or known him.

The NIV84 translates it:

No one who lives in him *keeps on sinning*. No one who *continues to sin* has either seen him or known him.

Another nearby verse that would support this interpretation is 1 John 3:9. The first half says:

No one who is born of God *practices sin*, because His seed abides in him; (NASB95)

This verse has another expression in Greek, ἁμαρτίαν οὐ ποιεῖ, which translated literally means, "does not do sin" or "does not practice sin."

EXERCISES

a. Practice with the PowerPoint exercises on *Thirdmill* or *LaBibliaaFondo*. (See the Preface for the addresses.) Click on "11 Verbs, Part 2".

b. Write the meaning of the grammatical terms:

active voice

Greek and Exegesis

passive voice

middle voice

deponent verbs

aorist tense

genitive absolute

c. Explain the significance of the moods in Greek verbs.

Mood	Significance
Indicative	
Subjunctive	
Imperative	
Infinitive	
Participle	

d. Take into account the meaning of the root verb and the morphological information and translate the following verbs:

τηρῆσετε

It comes from τηρέω, meaning "keep." It is in the form of future, active indicative, 2nd person plural.

Translation: _____

λαβεῖν

It comes from λαμβάνω, meaning "receive" or "take." It is in the form of an aorist active infinitive.

Translation: _____

ἦν

It comes from ἐιμί, meaning "to be." It is in the form of imperfect active indicative, 3rd person singular.

Translation: _____

ἑωράκαμεν

It comes from ὁράω, meaning "see." It is in the form of perfect active indicative, 1st person plural.

Translation: _____

πιστεύων

It comes from πιστεύω, meaning "believe". It is in the form of a present active participle, nominative masculine singular.

Translation: _____

e. Using *e-Sword* or *Logos*, find the information about the following verbs in John 3:26, including voice and mood, then write the translation:

ἔδωκεν

ἀπόληται

ἔχῃ

f. Make sure you practice the vocabulary again with the PowerPoint exercises on *Thirdmill* or *LaBibliaaFondo.* (See the Preface for the addresses.) Click on "10 Vocabulary List #5".

EXEGESIS ASSIGNMENT #6: ANALYSIS OF VERBS

The steps for analyzing the verbs in the Greek New Testament are similar to the steps for analyzing nouns and other parts of speech. Use this assignment guide to fill out the information in your "Exegesis Report".

Using *Logos* to Analyze Verbs

1. Open the "Exegetical guide," write the reference to the passage you are studying in the search box, and find the verbs in each verse in the section "Word by Word."

2. Investigate the key verbs in your passage.

3. You can see the root form of the verbs, listen to how they are pronounced, see the person, number, tense and mood. You can also learn more about the different meanings of the verbs by looking them up in the dictionaries listed.

Using *e-Sword* to Analyze Verbs

1. Find your passage in the Greek NT WH+.

2. Pass the mouse over the code above the key verbs you want to analyze.

3. Identify the tense, voice, mood, person and number of the verbs.

4. Click on the Strong's number and learn more about the different meanings of the verbs by looking them up in dictionaries such as Thayer.

10. Conjunctions and Syntax

10.1. Conjunctions

Conjunctions are words that unite, such as "and," "or," and "therefore." They are used very often to make complex sentences and to connect one sentence with another. Often these little words are important for understanding a Bible passage and its relation to the nearby context.

The Greek conjunctions that we have learned so far are:

γάρ	for, since, then
δέ	and, but
ἵνα	so that, that
καί	and
οὖν	therefore
οὕτως	thus

10.2 Syntax

Syntax is the structure of a sentence. It demonstrates the relationships between words and between phrases. Sentences are made complex in various ways. For example, a subject or verb can have more than one part. In that case, the parts are joined by a conjunction. In the following sentence, "and" is a conjunction that joins "the man" and "his wife", making a compound subject.

A man and his wife read books.

The structure could be diagrammed as follows:

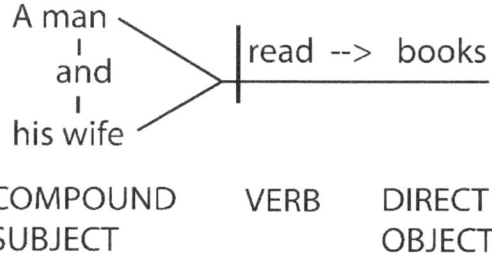

COMPOUND   VERB   DIRECT
SUBJECT   OBJECT

Greek sentences in the New Testament are often complex. Sometimes a conjunction joins two clauses. (In this book, we will use the definition of a clause as a group of words that contains a verb and expresses an idea.)

The man reads the Bible, and he loves it.

Here is a suggested diagram of the sentence:

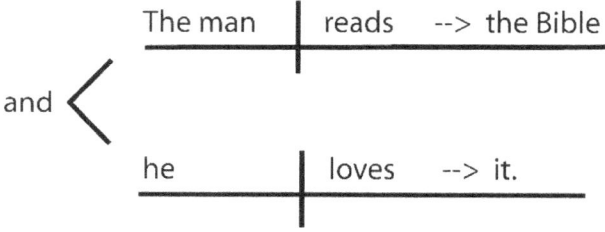

"The man" is the subject of the first clause, "reads" is the verb, and "the Bible is the direct object, because it receives the action. "And" is a conjunction that connects the two clauses. The subject of the second clause is "he," "loves" is the verb, and "it" is the direct object.

Some sentences are very complex, and it's difficult to diagram them. Note that an entire clause can function as a direct object of another clause or the subject of another clause. For example, suppose the sentence is:

Jesus said, "I am the Good Shepherd."

"Jesus" is the subject, "said" is the verb, and "I am the good shepherd" is a clause that functions as the direct object of the verb "said," because it indicates what it is that he said. In the second clause, "I" is the subject, "I am" is the verb, and "the Good Shepherd" is a predicate nominative, because it indicates who the subject is. The diagram could be as follows:

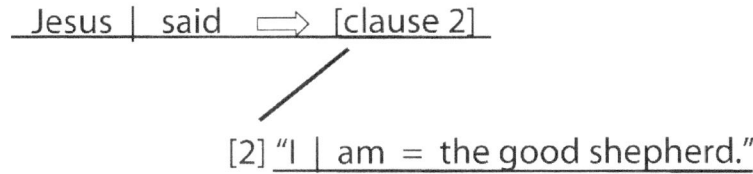

Jesus | said ⟹ [clause 2]

[2] "I | am = the good shepherd."

10.3. 2 Peter 1:1

It's very revealing to analyze the syntax of 2 Peter 1:1, because it is evidence of the deity of Jesus.

2 Peter 1:1
Simeon Peter, a servant and apostle of Jesus Christ, to those who have obtained a faith of equal standing with ours by the righteousness of our God and Savior Jesus Christ.

Notice in Greek that there is only one article introducing the phrase.

...τοῦ θεοῦ ἡμῶν καὶ σωτῆρος Ἰησοῦ Χριστοῦ

It doesn't say, "...by the righteousness *of* our God *and of* our Savior Jesus Christ" but "...by the righteousness *of* our God and Savior Jesus Christ." Grammatically, it points to the fact that both "our God" and "Savior" refer to Jesus Christ. A.T. Robertson says, "So the one article (*tou*) with *theou* and *sōtēros* requires precisely ...one person, not two."[36] This one person is the second person of the Trinity; He is our God, He is the Savior, and He is Jesus Christ!

10.4. Syntax of John 3:16

We could make a diagram of John 3:16 like the following. Notice how the conjunctions connect the clauses of the complex sentence.

---

[36] Robertson, A. (1997). *Word Pictures in the New Testament*. Vol. V c1932, Vol.VI c1933 Sunday School Board of the Southern Baptist Convention. (2 Pe 1:1). Oak Harbor: Logos Research Systems.

For...

[1] <u>God</u> | <u>loved</u> ⟹ <u>the world</u>
             ⌐ so

⋮ that

[2] <u>he</u> | <u>gave</u> ⟹   <u>son</u>
                 ⌐ his only

⋮ so that

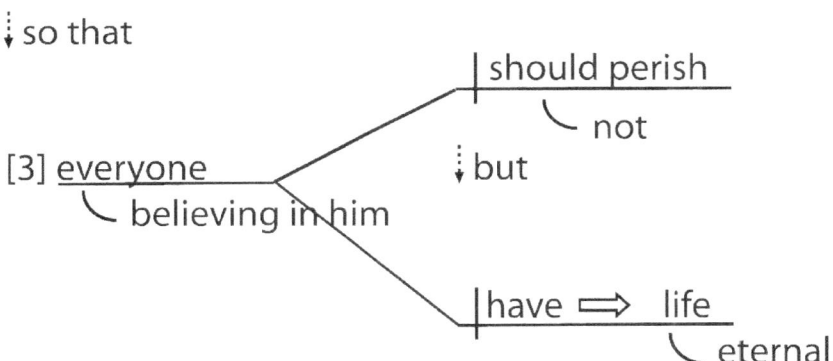

                    | should perish
                          ⌐ not
[3] <u>everyone</u>   ⋮ but
    ⌐ believing in him

                    | have ⟹ life
                           ⌐ eternal

EXEGESIS ASSIGNMENT #7: CONJUNCTIONS AND SYNTAX

The steps for analyzing the conjunctions in the Greek New Testament are similar to the steps for analyzing nouns, verbs, and other parts of speech. Use this assignment guide to fill out the information in your "Exegesis Report".

Using *Logos* to Analyze Conjunctions

1. Open the "Exegetical guide" to your passage and find the conjunctions in "Word by Word."

2. Look them up in a dictionary to confirm the different meanings and uses.

Using *e-Sword* to Analyze Conjunctions

1. Find your passage in the Greek NT WH+.

2. Pass the cursor over the code above the key verbs you want to analyze.

Identify the tense, voice, mood, person and number of the verb.

3. Click on the Strong's number and learn more about the different meanings of the verb by looking it up in dictionaries such as Thayer.

Syntax

Analyze the sentence structure of your passage. Try to identify the main clause (or the main clauses, if there is more than one sentence). Look for parallelism. Look for comparison and contrast. Look for any other keys to the structure of your passage. Make a simple diagram of each sentence to show the main structure.

Translation

Taking into account all the linguistic information you have accumulated during your study, compare the main translations you have seen and analyze why they have translated it this way. Then write what you consider to be the most accurate translation. It may be different from any translation you have read.

11. ANALYSIS OF THE BIBLICAL AND THEOLOGICAL IMPLICATIONS

Now you have completed the first three steps of exegesis. There are two remaining steps:

- ✓ 1) Ask questions about the passage.
- ✓ 2) Analyze the original context.
- ✓ 3) Analyze the linguistic meaning.
- **4) Analyze the biblical and theological implications.**
- **5) Apply the message in the present context.**

In this lesson, you will learn to interpret the passage biblically and theologically. This is a time for reflection and meditation. Ask the Holy Spirit to guide you. When you finish the lesson, you will write down your own reflections on your passage

There are three aspects to this process:

a. Reflect on how the passage fits in the whole Bible.

b. Read good commentaries on the passage to compare ideas.

c. Summarize the main message of the passage in your own words.

11.1. Reflect on how the passage fits in the whole Bible.

Now that you understand the linguistic meaning of the passage and have your own translation, reflect on how the passage fits in the whole Bible. Try to understand the meaning of the passage in its historical context. Does your present understanding of the passage seem to contradict another Bible passage? Does it contradict another important doctrine? Try to harmonize it with the rest of Scripture. Examine any parallel passage again to see if they help understand your passage. Look for any other passages related to the topic. Think about the context of redemption. Consider how this passage relates to the Old Testament. Consider how it relates to the rest of the New Testament. What does this passage teach us about Jesus and salvation? Write down your thoughts and answers.

Ask yourself other questions. What are other biblical and theological questions that arise? If you are studying John 3:16, you might have questions such as: What does it really mean to "believe" in Jesus? What is "eternal life"?

11.2. Read good commentaries.

You may wonder why we have waited until now to read commentaries. The reason is that we want you discover on your own the meaning of the passage before reading what others say. If you read the commentaries first, you will lose the benefit of your own original research. The commentaries can be gravely mistaken, and it might send you on the wrong path from the beginning, or the commentaries might just leave out some important aspects. We want you to become a faithful expositor of the passage you are studying, and not to simply quote other authors. However, now that you have already arrived at your own (at least tentative) conclusions go ahead and read some commentaries and theological books to see what they say. Talk to a person that you trust and ask him or her to recommend good books.

Remember to always keep Christ in the center of your thoughts and reflect on how your passage fits in the plan of salvation. Jesus is the "the way, the truth, and the life." Somehow all truth revolves around Him.

11.3. Summarize the main message of the passage.

You have studied the original context of your passage, and you have done a linguistic analysis of it. You have done your own translation of the passage and reflected on the biblical and theological implications. Now is the moment to ask yourself, "What is the main point of the passage?" We are not talking about the translation, and we are not looking for applications yet, but seeking the principal message of the passage. Think about how the first readers would have understood it. What did it mean for them? Explain it as concisely as you can in your own words.

12. APPLICATION OF THE MESSAGE IN THE PRESENT CONTEXT

In this lesson, you will learn to make the application of the message of a biblical passage in your own life and in the life of others in your context. When you finish, you will write down appropriate applications for your selected passage.

Making an application of a Bible passage is like moving from one country to another. Crossing geographical boundaries means you need to learn the language of the people, and you need to understand their culture and way of thinking. The biblical message was given originally to people that lived in a world quite different from ours. Once we understand what the message meant to the original hearers, and once we understand our current audience, we try to help them hear the same message. Contextualization can be complicated, because there are many diverse cultures. Every country is different, every city is different, and every church is different. In fact, every person is different.

CONTEXTUALIZATION

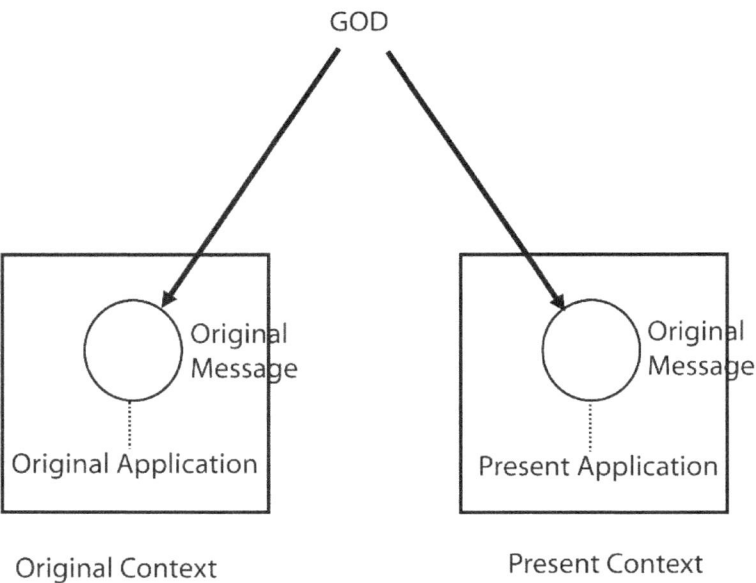

If we don't apply the message of a passage, we still don't understand it fully. In the biblical sense, you don't really "know" the truth fully until you live it. This is where our studies cease to be abstract reflections.

12.1. Reflect on the present context.

Analyze the context in which you live: yourself, your family, your church congregation, the neighborhood around your church, and the surrounding society in general. Much of this is the natural result of talking with people, even more importantly from listening to people. But we also need to make a conscious effort to understand the neighborhood. We can do surveys to discover the religious views and the needs of the people in our community. What are the needs and concerns of people around us, in our church or at our office? What are young people struggling with? What is happening in the families?

Sometimes our churches become self-centered. We expect people to come to us and become like us, instead of going out to "make disciples of all nations" (all ethnic groups). We are often out of touch with what is happening outside our own Christian circles. Take some time to investigate and reflect on the world we live in. What do the songs, the movies, and the television programs convey? What do the artists and philosophers have to say?

As we think of how to apply John 3:16, for example, we may discover that many people have a pantheistic concept of God. Others may consider God to be an impersonal force. Our passage, on the contrary, shows that God is a personal loving God and that He exists apart from His creation.

Others have an erroneous concept of faith. They might think it is enough to believe that God exists, or that Jesus was a wonderful man. Others think faith is an irrational blind leap against reason. Even some people in the church are confused, thinking it is sufficient to have "accepted Christ" by going forward in an evangelistic service. While many people are truly saved in a moment like this, the act of raising your hand or going forward does not necessarily mean you have true saving faith.

As for the concept of eternal life, many people hold to an oriental concept of reincarnation. Others believe that when you die, there is nothing more. John 3:16 and the surrounding verses indicate that some people will have eternal life and others will perish.

12.2. Practical applications

Finally, we look for concrete practical applications. All of our efforts to analyze the passage should end with some kind of spiritual blessing, with some positive change. What should I do to respond to the truths of this passage? How should I change my way of living, thinking or feeling? Ask for the Lord's guidance.

12.3. A sermon or Bible Study

The fruit of our studies can now be turned into a sermon or Bible study. Repackage the message for your audience, focusing on the main application. Begin with an introduction to get their attention. They often come with their minds on other things and need to be attracted to the message by speaking to them about something related to their daily lives. Mention the questions you had about the passage, then explain the answers you have found. Summarize the main point of the passage and make one or two key applications. Finally, conclude with something they will not forget, an illustration or a story that drives home the main point.

Application

- ✓ 1) Ask questions about the passage.
- ✓ 2) Analyze the original context.
- ✓ 3) Analyze the linguistic meaning.
- ✓ 4) Analyze the biblical and theological implications.
- ✓ 5) Apply the message in the present context.

EXEGESIS ASSIGNMENT #8:
BIBLICAL THEOLOGY, APPLICATION

Analyze the passage biblically and theologically.

1. Reflect and meditate on your passage and answer the following questions:

- Does your current understanding of the passage seem to contradict another Bible passage? Explain why.
- Does it contradict another important doctrine? Explain how.
- How does this passage relate to the Old Testament?
- What does this passage teach us about Jesus and salvation?
- Any other question?

2. Read 3 or 4 commentaries on your passage and write down any important thoughts or new discoveries.

3. Explain the main point of the passage in your own words.

Apply the message in the current context.
1. Write down important aspects of the context in which you live that are related to the message of your passage.
2. Write practical, concrete applications for yourself, your family, your congregation, and others. What should I do, think,

or feel as a result of my exegesis? What should I encourage others to do, think or feel?

    3. Write an outline and some main points for a sermon or Bible study.

EXEGESIS REPORT

ASSIGNMENT #1: Select your passage and ask questions.

1. Reference of passage:

2. Passage in favorite translation:

3. Why did you choose this passage? Do you have any doubts about it?

4. What are the differences in translations? Write down any phrases where there are important differences.

5. Do you have other questions about the passage?

6. What do you hope to learn from the study of this passage?

7. Note any thoughts from commentaries that call your attention initially.

ASSIGNMENT #2: Analyze the original context.

a. The historical context

1. Author of the book:

2. Estimated date of composition:

3. Situation of the people of God (the churches) at the time:

4. Important events surrounding the time of composition:

b. The literary context

1. Important verses surrounding the passage:

2. Main topics in the chapter or paragraph:

3. Literary genre of the book:

4. Main purpose of the book:

5. Important themes of the book:

6. Why do you think the Lord communicated this passage to the original audience?

ASSIGNMENT #3: Semantics (Word study)

1. Copy and paste the Greek text of your passage:

2. Practice reading the passage out loud in Greek.

3. Copy key Greek words and write down the possible meanings you have found in the dictionaries:

4. If you find something interesting about the use of the word in other passages, write down your observations and thoughts:

5. Write down what you consider the best translation of the key words. Remember that the near literary context is very important in determining the meaning of a word.

ASSIGNMENT #4: Analyze the nouns.

1. Using *e-Sword* or *Logos*, identify all the nouns in your passage. Make a list, copying the words from your Greek passage. Write down the case, number, and grammatical gender of each.

2. Identify the use of nouns in your passage. Write next to each one if they are subjects, direct objects, indirect objects, or predicate nominatives.

ASSIGNMENT #5: Analyze the adjectives, adverbs, pronouns, and prepositions.

1.   Identify all the adjectives, adverbs, pronouns, and prepositions in your passage. Copy your passage in Greek and write "ADJ" below the adjectives, "ADV" below the adverbs, "Pron" below pronouns, and "Prep" below the prepositions.

2. Write down which noun or pronoun is modified by each adjective and which verb is modified by each adverb.

3. Make a brief list of any adjectives, adverbs, pronouns or prepositions that are important for understanding your passage. Make some notes about why they are important.

ASSIGNMENT #6: Analyze the verbs.

Copy the important Greek verbs from your passage and write the tense, mood, voice, number and person for each of them. For participles, note also the case and gender. Write the key definitions.

Assignment #7: Conjunctions, Syntax and Translation

Conjunctions and Syntax

1. List the important Greek conjunctions in your passage.

2. Note the importance of the conjunctions for understanding your passage.

3. Analyze the structure of your passage. Try to identify the main clause (or main clauses, if there is more than one sentence). If you can, make a diagram.

4. Finish the linguistic study of your passage. Make sure you have all the key words analyzed, especially the verbs, noting the meanings and the forms.

Translation

Decide how to best translate the passage. Look again at the translations you looked at when you began your study. Analyze why the translators phrased it that way. Choose which you consider the best version. If none of them are satisfactory to you, write your own translation. Don't forget to take the literary context into account when doing your translation.

Greek and Exegesis

ASSIGNMENT #8: Biblical-Theological Implications and Application

a. Questions:

1. Does your present understanding of the passage seem to contradict another Bible passage? Explain.

2. Does it contradict another important doctrine? Explain.

3. How does this New Testament passage relate to the Old Testament?

4. What does this passage teach us about Jesus and salvation?

5. Do you have any other questions?

b. Commentaries

Write down any important thoughts or new discoveries from commentaries.

c. The Main Point

Explain the main point of the passage in your own words.

d. Application of the Message in the Present Context

1. Write down important aspects of the context you live in that are related to the message of your passage.

2. Write down practical concrete applications for yourself, your family, your congregation and others. What should I do, think, or feel as a result of my exegesis? What should I encourage others to do, think or feel?

3. Write an outline for a sermon or Bible Study based on your passage and note some key thoughts you would include. Include ideas for illustrations, stories, and examples, especially for the introduction and the conclusion.

How to Prepare an Exegetical Essay

Sometimes an academic institution or a church requests an exegetical essay as part of a course or to fulfill requirements for ordination to the ministry. It is not the same as the more technical "Exegesis Report" that you have prepared above, giving the results of your research. The essay should be an article that presents the argument or defense of your interpretation of the passage. It is more academic than a sermon, but less detailed, than the "Exegesis Report." It should include an introduction, the body of the essay, and a conclusion.

The introduction
It should begin with an explanation of the difficulties of the passage. Explain why you have selected the passage and what you intend to solve. Awaken the reader's interest by showing the importance of gaining a correct interpretation of the passage. For example, as we show in this book, the verse James 2:24 could give the impression that salvation is achieved by good works. However, there are other passages that say the opposite. How can we resolve this apparent contradiction?

The body
This section presents the main content of the essay. It usually has several subsections.

A. It could begin by explaining the different interpretations that have been given of the passage. You could cite some comments and possibly explain the perspectives of different churches or theological perspectives, noting what you consider to be right or wrong. For example, the Roman Catholic perspective of James 2:24 could be very different from the Protestant perspective.

B. You could follow with an explanation of the results of your own exegetical research. It should not include all the details, but only the most important things. It might include something about the original context of the passage and some of the more important aspects of your linguistic analysis. For example, as we saw in the book, it could explain the different meanings of the word δικαιόω (dikaióô), normally translated "justify" in the verse.

The conclusion

You could end with a practical, contextualized application. What is the significance of this passage? For example, it makes a big difference whether we believe that salvation is by works or by faith alone. It is also important to prove that there are no contradictions in the Bible.

This is just an example. The exegetical essay should show what you have learned in your research. The important thing is to highlight the importance of resolving any doubts about the interpretation of the passage and the practical application.